DIALOGUES
for
DIVERSITY

This book was bound using
the RepKover™ process,
which creates a special
lie-flat binding.

RepKover
OTABIND

DIALOGUES
for
DIVERSITY

Community and Ethnicity on Campus

The Project on Campus Community and Diversity
of the Accrediting Commission
for Senior Colleges and Universities
of the Western Association of
Schools and Colleges

Martin Kramer and Stephen S. Weiner,
Co-Directors

Made Possible by a Grant
from The James Irvine Foundation

ORYX PRESS
1994

The rare Arabian Oryx is believed to have inspired the myth of the unicorn. This desert antelope became virtually extinct in the early 1960s. At that time several groups of international conservationists arranged to have 9 animals sent to the Phoenix Zoo to be the nucleus of a captive breeding herd. Today the Oryx population is over 800, and nearly 400 have been returned to reserves in the Middle East.

Copyright © 1994 by the Accrediting Commission for Senior Colleges and Universities of the Western Association of Schools and Colleges
Published by The Oryx Press
4041 North Central at Indian School Road
Phoenix, Arizona 85012-3397

Published simultaneously in Canada

Printed and Bound in the United States of America

∞ The paper used in this publication meets the minimum requirements of American National Standard for Information Science—Permanence of Paper for Printed Library Materials, ANSI Z39.48, 1984.

Library of Congress Cataloging-in-Publication Data
Dialogues for diversity: community and ethnicity on campus / The
   Project on Campus Community and Diversity of the Accrediting
   Commission for Senior Colleges and Universities of the Western
   Association of Schools and Colleges, Martin Kramer and
   Stephen S. Weiner, co-directors.
      p.   cm.—(American Council on Education / Oryx series on higher
   education)
   Includes bibliographical references and index.
   ISBN 0-89774-867-0
   1. Minority college students—United States. 2. Community and
college—United States. 3. Multicultural education—United States.
4. United States—Ethnic relations. I. Kramer, Martin, 1932 Dec.
11– II. Weiner, Stephen (Stephen S.) III. Western Association of
Schools and Colleges (U.S.). Accrediting Commission for Senior
Colleges and Universities. IV. Series.
LC3727.064 1993
378.1'9829'073—dc20   93-31063
                                                              CIP

TABLE OF CONTENTS

> *TOPIC ONE:*
> *MISSION AND*
> *DIVERSITY*

TOPIC TWO: THE SOCIAL CONTEXT

> *TOPIC THREE:*
> *DIVERSITY AND*
> *QUALITY*

> *TOPIC FOUR:*
> *COMMUNITY AND*
> *CAMPUS CLIMATE*

TOPIC FIVE:
STUDENT DEVELOPMENT
AND ETHNIC IDENTITY

PREFACE

This is *not* yet another book arguing the case or acknowledging the importance of ethnic diversity for the future of American higher education. That case has been made, and eloquently, by many others. These materials are, rather, intended to help groups of individuals on campus toward focused discussions of the role of ethnic diversity in the daily life of colleges and universities. The aim is to help such groups to find their own common ground, not to tell them what that common ground should be.

Consider one view:

> Diversity is about how "us" and "them" are defined, how "we" separate ourselves from "others" and how such distinctions impact upon human life. The differences are manifold—indeed, they include all the possible groupings of individuals by characteristics they share or do not share. At its core the discussion of diversity in higher education calls upon us to revisit questions about the skills and sensitivities needed for constructive relations among people who are different, the principles that animate a just and democratic society, and the variety of knowledge that is important for scholars both to seek and to teach. The gift that diversity gives is the insistent invitation to ask hard questions about what we mean by education, how we teach, which people should be included as students and teachers, and what we are accomplishing in our colleges and universities. If we let it, diversity can renew our campuses.

Such a statement brings forth powerful reactions, causing us to ask ourselves:

> How do I respond, both intellectually and emotionally, to these issues? Do I agree or disagree? What are my facts and what are my assumptions?

> Do I usually think of diversity as the kind of gift described, or more often as a difficult problem that threatens valued kinds of stability?

> Would I and my institution do a better job if we found more occasions to remind ourselves that diversity is a gift?

These are the kinds of questions that people connected with colleges and universities need to talk about with each other more candidly than they usually do. But a good many worries, some uncomfortable to talk about, can get in the way:

Will standards of academic freedom and quality, at least as we have known them, be sacrificed?

Will faculty and administration lose control of our institutions to hostile, outside forces?

Will systematic discrimination against White males replace the exclusionary practices of the past?

Will diversity foster separatism, and will our campus fragment into hostile camps?

Both the questions and the worries need to be discussed. This volume is designed to help such discussion get started.

We can gain confidence in dealing with the questions and the worries from the quiet achievements that diversity has already brought, such as the following:

- a sense of pride on the part of many individuals whose group identification previously denied it

- the flowering of talent among people whose parents did not have the chance to gain education and develop their talents fully

- the growth of friendships and working relationships that cross lines of ethnicity and other lines of difference

- the new scholarship that has come to many disciplines as the result of the provocative perspectives brought by diversity

- the wider sharing of knowledge and human experience, culture and sensibilities, different from those students and faculty previously understood

- greater attention to the moral dimensions of thought and action as the contrasting assumptions of different cultures have come into sharper relief

- a stronger capacity, both personal and institutional, to move from conflict to trust

These achievements have enabled us to understand that in multicultural and multiracial communities there are options besides those of total assimilation or strict segregation. Students, faculty, and staff can maintain significant ethnic affiliations and friendships while leading lives that include frequent, and rewarding, crossing of ethnic lines both in personal and professional domains.

Diversity has also taught us some lessons about the education of *all* students:

1. Students in general—and *not only* ethnic minority students—are much more vulnerable to hurt and discouragement than past academic practice has usually recognized.

2. Almost any casually grouped set of students (as in a typical class-room) includes individuals who come with a variety of learning styles and a variety of experiences available to connect with any given topic or subject matter. The presence of ethnic minority students has made faculty much more aware that this is the case for *all* students.

3. There is no such thing as a culturally disengaged student any more than there is such a thing as a purely economic man. The values and organizing principles of an individual student's cultural identity are the source of much of the student's energy and ability to focus that energy on tasks of personal and intellectual growth.

4. The variety of student cultures provides a richness of contrasts and contexts for the intellectual growth of *all* students that is new and immensely valuable. The kind of cosmopolitanism that some colleges and universities laboriously promote—by, in effect, importing cultural enrichment and global education—is now on campus simply by virtue of the presence of the new students. It is a gift, not an expensive add-on.

Diversity has indeed turned out to be a gift, not solely for those with a particular skin color, physical appearance, or gender. It is a gift from all to all. "Diversity" is a word that has rapidly acquired many meanings. Central to these many meanings, however, are three defining aspects of a diverse college or university: (1) members of groups previously excluded from full, fair, and respected participation in higher education are present on campus as full participants; (2) the campus itself provides a supportive community environment that values such participation and is conducive to its success; and (3) the institution recognizes the value of the groups with which students and faculty identify as sources of important intellectual perspectives and personal support, and as avenues of participation in universal human concerns.

These three conditions help define the scope of the dialogues these materials are intended to stimulate. They concern hopes and opportunities that are not new to our society. Professor Robert Cottrol of the School of Law of Rutgers University has observed:

> For all its faults and for all the faults that a multi-cultural education will uncover and report, the United States remains the most successful multi-ethnic and multiracial society of our time, perhaps of all time.
> . . . Perhaps our most important contribution to the twenty-first century will be to demonstrate that people from different races, cultures, and ethnic backgrounds can live side by side; retain their uniqueness; and, yet, over time form a new common culture. That has been the American story. It is a history that has much to tell the world. It must be told by American educators.
>
> (Cottrol, R. "America the Multicultural." *The American Educator* [Winter 1990]: 2+.)

The kind of discussion envisioned by these materials may well be a useful starting point for a campus self-study of diversity issues solely for institutional purposes or in connection with the accreditation process. These *Dialogues* do not, however, prescribe that process or discuss accreditation standards. Our accrediting commission has stated its positions on those matters elsewhere.* The role of the commission in connection with these *Dialogues* has been to sponsor the efforts that have gone into their preparation as a service to member institutions, not as a mandate. The James Irvine Foundation has generously provided the financial support for these efforts.

We wish to thank all those who joined in the preparation of these materials through their ideas, criticisms, and suggestions. Their names are listed on the following page. In particular, appreciation is due to Raymond F. Bacchetti, a member of the commission from 1985 to 1992, and chair of the commission from 1989 to 1992, for his critical role in launching and nurturing this effort, and to Martin Kramer, who has endeavored to put the insights of many people into printed words. We also wish to thank the students, faculty, and staff of California State University, Fresno; California State University, Long Beach; and Loma Linda University who have participated in discussions using draft materials for this volume. We have learned much of value from their experiences.

> *Donald R. Gerth*
> President, California State University, Sacramento
> Chair, Accrediting Commission for Senior Colleges
> and Universities of the Western Association of
> Schools and Colleges
>
> *Stephen S. Weiner*
> Executive Director, Accrediting Commission for
> Senior Colleges and Universities

---

*The Commission's Policy Statement on Diversity is available at the Commission office: P.O. Box 9990, Mills College, Oakland, CA 94613-0990.

Participants in the Development of Dialogues for Diversity

James Appleton
Tomás Arciniega
Gail Auletta
Raymond Bacchetti
Edgar Beckham
B. Lyn Behrens
Nancy Bekavac
Alfred H. Bloom
Aubrey W. Bonnett
Patrick Callan
Desdemona Cardoza
Trevor Chandler
Doris Ching
Stanley Chodorow
Sister Magdalen Coughlin
Troy Duster
Penny Edgert
Richard Foth
Russell Garth
Donald R. Gerth
Reverend Thomas Gleeson
Madeleine J. Goodman
Milton Gordon
Roberto P. Haro
Neil Hoffman
Francisco Jimenez
Terry Jones
Sister Kathleen Kelly
Martin Kramer
Richard Kriegbaum
Steven D. Lavine
Maxine Leeds
Reverend Paul Locatelli
Raymond Lou
John Maguire
Curtis McCray

Janet McKay
Jere Mock
Stephen Morgan
Andrea Morrison
Yolanda Moses
Caryn McTighe Musil
Don T. Nakanishi
Carol Niehus
Morgan Odell
John R. O'Neil
Arturo Pacheco
Douglas Patiño
Karl S. Pister
Norma Rees
Richard Richardson
Henry E. Riggs
Agnes C. Robinson
Michael Rodriguez
Theodore Saenger
Jack Schuster
Sister Veronica Skillin
Daryl Smith
Marilyn Snider
Peter W. Stanley
Nancy Stark
Joseph Subbiondo
Lucille Tenazas
Peter Thigpen
Joseph W. Watson
Stephen S. Weiner
John Welty
Sandra Wilcox
David Winter
Ralph Wolff
Frank F. Wong

A Note to Users

The purpose of these materials is to offer some starting points for serious conversation about ethnic diversity on campus. Declaring this purpose will immediately prompt the question: How can faculty, students, and administrators possibly need such materials? Are they not the most articulate people in our society, engaged every day in conversations of the most wide-ranging and demanding sort? How can *they* need *help*?

The answer is that talking about ethnic diversity on campus makes some extraordinary demands on people. If these conversations are to accomplish very much, the means must be found for people to set aside temporarily their highly engaged positions. Some participants may need to descend from elaborately defended intellectual fortresses. Some may need to free themselves from an exaggerated decorum that is intended to avoid giving offense, but that often, in fact, stifles conversation. It is further necessary to set aside a natural wish to seek definitive solutions to institutional problems. Agendas, and the verbal tactics that get agendas adopted, need to be put "on hold."

Why do these positions and attitudes need to be set aside? Because they can all be impediments to listening and, in turn, responding to what others are really saying. What is it that for this other person is of sharp, central, and illuminating importance, although to me it has always seemed a vague, trivial, or peripheral matter? What are the tests of fairness, relevance, and respect that this other person applies to issues of ethnic diversity, perhaps quite different tests from mine? How might I paraphrase what the other person has said in my own language, as corollaries of my own principles? How does this other person respond in turn? And what feelings of hurt or hope seep through the exchange, from both sides? Defensive and political concerns need to be set aside so that people can more easily listen for answers to such questions.

The kind of conversation envisaged here is both practical and not. It is not practical in the sense that it does not aim at making decisions about action or the kind of policy that might be codified in an institution's handbook. Indeed, a good deal of distance from such matters is important for people to be able to say what they have to say without threatening the positions of others. To provide such distance is precisely the reason for offering in these materials so many fictitious case studies, "thought experiments," and dialogues.

Yet at the same time, the kind of conversation envisaged here is intensely practical. A full and sweeping consensus is perhaps very unlikely to emerge, but mutual understanding about at least a few important premises for future action is quite possible. This is because the participants will have learned more about the experiences and perceptions that such premises need to take into account. The participants are also likely to have groped their way toward a common language for articulating these premises and communicating about them. It is reasonable to hope that an articulate sensitivity will have gained ground on a sterile decorum in dealing with issues of ethnic diversity.

A variety of discussion materials are included in this volume:

- extended case studies
- short case studies and exercises termed "thought experiments"
- dialogues termed "dilemmas"
- topical essays
- quotations from students, faculty members, and administrators termed "voices of experience"

The voices of experience are the words of real people, but the case studies and dilemmas are fictional, with one exception (called here "Midwestern University," see p. 100). Of course, the invented situations are not fully imaginary in that elements of the fictional situations can be observed on real college and university campuses. However, the materials intentionally describe institutions that are explicitly *not* the institution from which discussion participants are drawn, to allow participants enough distance so they will not be inhibited from saying how they would really view the situation presented. There is valuable cover in discussing a hypothetical case.

Printed discussion materials are but one ingredient in the kind of conversation needed. The final section of these materials, "Planning and Conducting Discussions of Ethnic Diversity," offers suggestions on how the many other ingredients can be assembled and combined to lay the basis for constructive discussion. That section is lengthy, going into a good deal of detail about practices that will support candid communication. The detail seems called for because it can too easily happen that a good conversation is frustrated by any one of many possible small obstructions that could have been avoided if they had been thought about in advance. Thoughtful planning is essential. We urge those who have the responsibility of organizing discussions to read and consider the suggestions made in the last section, although there may well be less need for other participants in a discussion group to do so.

What the other members of a group may want to do is to think a little about the kind of participants they want to be. Each of you really does have something to contribute when you enter the room. This something may be lost if you take the usual kinds of passive or contentious roles. For example, you may have the habit of taking detailed notes. This habit can make you a member of an audience, rather than a full participant. It may be better to take notes only of points that will help you to respond actively to what others are saying and to join in the group's evaluation of how all its members are working together.

Again, it is for many academics almost habitual to try to be brilliant or witty or both. Perhaps such a habit needs to be under a bit more control than usual. On the other hand, some controls may need to be relaxed a bit. You, like many academics, may have the habit of suppressing or distancing yourself from any idea for which you cannot immediately offer compelling evidence or arguments. Why not instead let the other participants help you sort out which of your ideas are most worthwhile, just as you can help them? An internal censorship that enjoins silence before this sorting out can even begin will diminish both your individual contribution and the group's achievement.

The result of carrying on a conversation under this kind of regime of candor may, of course, be that you hear others saying some fairly outrageous things or that you find yourself saying them. It may be almost a reflex to react combatively or defensively when this happens. It would be better to think both of what others say and what you say yourself as raw material for the group's process of inquiry.

What, then, is the kind of good discussion of which you want to be a part? We suggest the following criteria, repeated in the concluding section of this volume:

1. Are people talking about what seems to them genuinely important?

2. Do people respond in ways that show that they are really listening?

3. Are people expressing themselves in more than usually candid ways, because they sense that the other participants are respectful and reflective listeners, even if they are inclined to disagree?

4. Are difficult issues being discussed for the first time or in a more constructive way than usual?

5. Does the discussion "take off," with successive speakers bringing forth observations that build on those that have gone before?

6. Does the discussion seem to point in the direction of new areas of agreement, even if the terms of that agreement would be very hard to formulate?

7. Do members of the group show an inclination to prolong discussions, to meet again, or to find a way to involve others in similar discussions?

If the members of a group are making the effort of looking for this kind of discussion, they can expect to find it.

A Note on Terminology

A comment about some issues of terminology is in order. Our dictionary (*American Heritage Dictionary of the English Language*. Boston, MA: American Heritage Publishing / Houghton Mifflin, 1969) defines *race* as "a local geographic or global human population distinguished as a more or less distinct group by genetically transmitted physical characteristics." *Ethnic* is defined as "Of or pertaining to a social group within a cultural and social system that claims or is accorded special status on the basis of complex, often variable traits including religious, linguistic, ancestral or physical characteristics. Broadly, characteristics of a religious, racial, national, or cultural group." We have used both terms in these materials, but we use *ethnicity* more often, allowing as it does for more complex identifications.

A further problem of terminology concerns use of the term *minority* for any of the racial or ethnic groups that have been historically underrepresented in American higher education. In a purely arithmetical sense this term is descriptive of any one such group if it does not constitute a majority. Yet, for some people, the term *minority* carries the sense of marginalization—*not counting* where important needs, interests, and contributions are concerned. For this reason, some people prefer the term *people of color*. However, this term is in turn objectionable to many, because there are important distinctions among the groups to which it refers, not to mention differences among the many communities broadly grouped together as Latino, Asian, Native, or African Americans.

In these materials we have not adopted any one terminology, and we have not tried to be consistent throughout. This is partly because terminology is one of the things that needs to be discussed in the conversations these materials attempt to stimulate. Being prescriptive about such a matter would be at odds with that intention. Further, there are situations where the openness of a term can itself be an advantage. For example, there are occasions where the term *minority* in the discussion materials can give the user the option of choosing to address issues related to a group of Asian *or* Latino *or* Native *or* African Americans.

DIALOGUES
for
DIVERSITY

MISSION
AND
DIVERSITY

1

CASES

Three cases are offered for discussion of issues connecting ethnic diversity with institutional mission. The first case, Parrales State University, presents some of the circumstances of the large, urban, public institutions that an increasing percentage of students attend. This is not, however, the only kind of institution challenged by diversity. Woods College and Forest College encounter diversity in very different circumstances—respectively, those of a small Protestant college and those of a liberal arts college in the great books tradition.

PARRALES STATE UNIVERSITY

The mission of Parrales State University is to serve a student body that is mostly commuter, mostly part-time. Through its students, Parrales serves a variety of ethnic communities. Parrales is considering an update of its graduation requirements.

Parrales State University is located in a community that started on the road to urbanization as a Latino settlement whose first inhabitants were small farmers. In succession, it became a railway terminus, an oasis for midwesterners fleeing the frosts of the Corn Belt, a dormitory suburb inhabited by many defense workers, and a new home for immigrants from Latin America and Asia.

Parrales' mission also reflects a process of accretion. To its original teacher-training mission have been added successively a full liberal arts baccalaureate program, engineering degrees, and a broad array of other bachelor's- and master's-level professional programs. Some of the programs have grown much more rapidly than others, but all have grown. Since the mid-1970s, most of the growth has come from the enrollment of older students, who usually have families, full-time jobs, or both. As a consequence, two-thirds of Parrales' students are enrolled less than full-time, and courses that meet evenings and weekends are chronically overenrolled. The university is dependent financially on these "nontraditional" students, both for the formula-funding their enrollment brings from the state and, increasingly, for their student fees.

Parrales has not, however, revised its formal mission statement since 1975, and the president has been considering the need for a new one. He has been having a good deal of trouble explaining to the trustees many of the apparently unconnected decisions he has been asking them to make. Why, they want to know, are they being asked to expand some programs while others are on short rations? What is the rationale for changing funding formulas, faculty work loads, and tenure procedures, each set of rules incorporating more exceptions and provisos than the last? A revised mission statement could, the president thought, make some sense of this chaos. It would also provide an occasion for an explicit recognition of Parrales' actual multiculturalism, from which springs a part, though only a small part, of the complexity.

The president has, however, a more immediate problem. The faculty senate has just given final approval to a new requirement of six credit hours in ethnic studies or world cultures for graduation. The senate listened responsively to all the concerned ethnic constituencies, and its leaders were convinced that the requirement was sensible and would, in practice, enable Parrales to avoid the usual charges of political correctness.

It turns out, however, that the resistance is much more mundane. It seems that a good many students have calculated the effect of the new requirement on the time it will take them to graduate, and many have come to the conclusion that enrollment for an additional semester will be necessary. Since most of Parrales' students are part-time and already are taking six to eight years to get their degrees, this could be a serious problem. The president asked several members of the cabinet group that advises Parrales on diversity matters what should be done about the protests.

> How should students be consulted, if at all, in establishing an ethnic studies requirement for graduation?

When asked, the provost was emphatic that the university should go ahead with the ethnic studies/world cultures requirement. She had that morning interviewed two candidates for after-school baby-sitting for her own children. Both of them had been referred by the student employment office. One was a not-so-young Black woman for whom this would be a second job in addition to a regular evening job. She had asked whether she could bring her own child with her in the afternoons, so that her husband could pick her up, drop her off at her other job, and look after the child in the evening himself. This woman was in exactly the kind of poignant situation that was cause for concern. She was already in her fifth year of part-time enrollment at the university with no degree in sight. She wanted to be a teacher, and the provost guessed from her openness and thoughtfulness about children that she could be a very good one. Yet it would be important that the university give her a better chance to connect her own difficult experience of the world with broader cultural horizons and with her professional development.

The other candidate for the job was a White woman who had separated recently from her companion of several years. This woman felt extremely isolated on campus and, indeed, in the urban environment as a whole. The provost wanted to give her a hug, but what she needed more than that was an education that would rekindle her curiosity, make sense of her opportunities, and enable her to see the people around her as enriching her world, not threatening it. It seemed that she would feel greatly relieved to get a job in a White household, and this suggested that her expectations of other ethnic groups in other settings triggered considerable anxiety.

Thinking about these two cases, the provost said, "I know there can be real anguish in postponing degree completion, so let's cut some other requirement. But I know students who need exactly the sense of dignity and perspective good multicultural courses can foster. Graduates should be able to say who they are, where they come from, and where they are going. A graduate should feel culturally connected, not isolated."

The vice-president for public affairs saw the problem differently. "It is not by adding things on that we will live up to our potential as a multicultural institution, least of all by adding hurdles to our graduation requirements that will hold people back. The need is not to change *what* we teach but *how* we teach it. What our students need is a sense of working together cross-culturally in class participation, study groups, and cocurricular projects."

In making these remarks, the vice-president was thinking of a breakfast meeting he had had that morning with a group of Asian-American business leaders who had been appointed to a regional business development committee. The particular concern these leaders expressed was the difficulty companies had in building a coherent work force recruited from the multilingual, multicultural local population. They asked what the university could do to help. The vice-president thought the university could do a good deal, but only by addressing similar issues among its own students, faculty, and staff. "A graduate of Parrales," he concluded, "should have the confidence and sensitivity to work out collaborative relationships in technically and culturally complex workplaces."

The dean of Humanities had different advice. "It is not only *how* we teach and learn that is important. Content is important too, and the ethnic studies requirement would recognize that. What the requirement doesn't do is deal with the fragmentation of the curriculum. Every course here, at least every humanities course, could and should have a multicultural perspective. Who knows, if it did, we might not need the new requirement."

In making these remarks, the dean was thinking of the list of new grant awards from the State Humanities Council she had just seen. None of the three applicants from Parrales had been among the winners. What this university needed, she thought, was some sense of the varied cultural resources the institution possessed and much more will to bring these resources together in a program that meant something to all its students, all its faculty. She was going to knock heads together, if she had to, to produce a single proposal for the next round of grants that would

> **?** Each member of the president's cabinet group takes a position in response to a recent experience. Would you see those experiences as pointing to proposals other than those the members of the group make?

represent a university-wide determination to make an integrated educational contribution with all these resources.

"A graduate," she concluded, "should have had the experience of understanding literature, and the people behind the literature, from multiple points of view. He or she should take from here an ability, more or less habitual, to do this as a mature adult."

The director of student services took yet a different tack. "The course requirement may or may not be too much to ask, but let's be clear about what it represents. It's an effort to use familiar academic means—graduation requirements—to make something happen: to make *community* happen. At our kind of institution we don't have athletics, social groups, and residence halls that do much to build community, so it is much harder for us than for others. But to find ways to give our loosely connected student body a sense of belonging to a learning community that can include all our ethnicities, all our social classes, all our public and private purposes in being here—that is something of the first importance. If ethnic studies helps, fine, but we should be prepared to do a lot of other things too."

The director was thinking of an odd experience he had had on his way to the meeting with the president that morning. His car had broken down, he had been afraid he would be late, and he had come to campus by taxi. The driver was Latino or Lebanese, probably both. He started talking about his experiences at the university when he heard the campus was their destination. It seemed he had dropped out six years ago when he had had to go home to see his dying father. He had never registered again, although he lived near the university and seemed to have depended on it for much of his social life.

Then the director suddenly remembered the case—it had crossed his desk when he was a student-aid administrator. On returning to the United States, this man's legal residency had suddenly become open to question, and he had been asked to pay back student aid he had received on the basis of his apparently quite sincere assumption that he was a U.S. citizen. The director wondered whether the university had not become, for this nearly stateless person, the nearest thing he knew to an accepting community, yet one that all the levels of bureaucracy prevented him from claiming as his own.

The director concluded, "A graduate should be able to make sense of a pretty crazy economic and social world. He needs to have had opportunities to be a member of a supportive multicultural community that will enable him to cope productively with that world."

The president had been taking notes as members of the group spoke. When they were finished he said,

> *What needs of particular students come to your mind in thinking about diversity as part of your mission?*

 *Is it possible to assess achievement of any of the educational goals advocated at Parrales?*

"You know, I'm not sure you have made the ethnic studies issue any easier to resolve. If we require it, it won't be enough; if we don't require it, we will have to find other ways to meet the objective. But what you *have* done is help me with a first draft of a new mission statement. I have written down the remarks each of you made, and they all belong in the preamble to our mission statement. To make good on the intent behind our graduation requirements is exactly what our mission is."

WOODS COLLEGE

Woods College, shaped by the culture and doctrine of a Bible-centered Protestant denomination, is considering whether to use a major gift to serve members of new congregations established by Central American immigrants.

Woods College was founded just before the turn of the century as the western seminary of a Protestant denomination that insists on the supreme authority of the Bible, but that also insists on a grace granted each redeemed person to interpret the message of the Bible in that person's own situation. The church has, as a result, experienced only a minimal number of doctrinal conflicts. Within a few years of the founding of Woods College, its program for preparing ministers was separated from its regular four-year undergraduate program. It has never, however, become an entirely secular college. All students are required to take Bible courses each year. Drinking and smoking are disciplinary matters of some seriousness. Dances, with chaperons, are permitted, but no social fraternity or sorority has been allowed, on the ground that their influence on student morals would be hard to control. A major annual event is "Missions Week," when missionaries who are alumni of the college return to talk about their experiences and to recruit new workers for the mission field.

About two-thirds of the students at Woods College are members of the church. These include some of the most academically gifted students, who prefer to attend the church's college rather than one of the highly selective colleges where they could easily gain admission. Most of the college's students, however, had only modest high school grades. There is no cut-off grade point average or minimum test score for admission. It has been a recruitment asset of the college that it can offer a four-year baccalaureate program with small classes on a very attractive campus to students whose only options among public institutions would be either a community college or a large, unselective state university. Woods College's other major asset is its clear commitment to moral and religious convictions.

The finances of Woods College reflect the importance of low tuition costs to its students' families, for few are rich or even upper middle class. They would generally prefer low tuition met from savings and earnings to higher tuitions partly given back as need-based aid. Some students have scholarships (termed "stewardships") awarded by individual congregations, but there is little other grant aid. Few students participate in the federal student loan programs before their junior or senior years.

Because of its low tuition policy, the college is very careful of expenses. Faculty salaries are low (in the bottom quartile in national rankings), and most faculty members are members of the church and regard their teaching as a calling. Food service and maintenance are performed without pay by students, under the supervision of a few paid profession-

Some Interim Questions

What factors are likely to make a commitment to ethnic diversity attractive or difficult for Woods to undertake?

What opportunities and obstacles for a diversity initiative do the traditions and commitments of your institution create?

als. Students also provide most clerical support in the library and in administrative offices. This work is paid, mainly from federal work-study funds. Even so, the college's financial position has at times been precarious. When the World War II GI Bill boom ended, the college was saved only by a large bequest from one of its (few) rich alumni.

Finances are again precarious, but another rich alumnus has appeared and is offering a large gift. The college is now in the process of deciding what to do with the money. There are a number of proposals:

1. The college should use the money to raise salaries and to become more academically selective, so that it will become, in fact and in image, a "good" liberal arts college.

2. The college should spend none of the money now. Colleges such as Woods are financially threatened from many sides. Gifts from individual congregations are not keeping up with inflation, and it is harder and harder to find faculty willing to accept low salaries. The college should adopt the policy of Joseph in Egypt, saving the windfalls of good years for the lean years ahead.

3. The college should launch a program in business administration. The traditional constituencies of the college would be comfortable with this initiative, and such an offering would help in recruiting students. If some such initiative is not undertaken, the college could soon face a crisis of declining enrollments.

4. The college should launch a program in nursing. This is an important calling for women students, and nurses are in even more short supply in the mission field than in the United States.

5. The college should use the money to recruit ethnic minority students and to establish programs that would enable them to be comfortable and to succeed at Woods College.

This final proposal has been made in response to a recently discovered fact. The church's missions in Central America have been highly successful, so that a good many of the recent immigrants from these countries have been either members of the church or very favorably disposed toward it. The college only recently discovered that these recent immigrants have founded two thriving congregations within 50 miles of the college. It is not clear how many of the young people will be graduating from high school or whether they or their parents have much of an idea of what going to college means in the United States. There is, however, a potential recruitment pool here, and an opportunity to serve members of the church whose involvement in American society is very preliminary and, from all indications, often painful and frightening. In line with the tradition of the church, it is widely felt that, as a matter of Christian conscience, the college should do something substantial to help.

Some Interim Questions

Which of the proposals would involve a change of Woods' mission?

If your institution, like Woods, had a major gift, what would be some of the other programs that would compete for resources with an effort to deepen the institution's engagement of diversity?

There are many reservations about "adopting" the new Central American constituency and investing money in it that could instead safeguard the college's future in other ways. These reservations are expressed, and discussed, as issues of conscience:

"We need to be sure that we would do good that would outweigh the good we would sacrifice. To our present students, this is a secure place that can be relied upon to live up to their very American expectations for a religiously oriented college experience. New students from a Central American background in more than token numbers would seem strange, and they *would* be strange. They would not know what to expect of us nor we of them."

"As a practical matter, we would have to become bilingual, in order to deal with the most everyday problems of students and their families. Are faculty and administrators really prepared to do this? We would be committing our energies as well as our money."

"Is it really defensible to make such an effort only on behalf of the Central Americans? We have never felt an obligation to make a special effort to recruit African Americans or Asian Americans, and we enroll very few."

"What would happen to the quality of the education we provide? Granted, we are not very demanding of GPAs and test scores. Still, we do take students of a not very academic turn of mind and equip them to be informed and thoughtful citizens, workers, and church members. This task absorbs our best energies. Taking on a new and difficult task would almost certainly mean less success in our traditional task."

"Is our church a sufficient tie with these people to give us assurance that we really do share the same way of looking at the world, on which so much that we do depends? We know that many in Central America joined Protestant churches such as ours as a kind of political protest against extremes of left and right. We belong to our church for quite different reasons, with different implications."

"Would this just be the beginning of a process that would undermine our witness? What if the next step was to accommodate people who do not accept the Bible as the authoritative plan for ordering our relations with God and one another? How do we draw the line between cultural accommodation and loss of vision?"

Some Concluding Questions for Discussion

In its thinking about the Central Americans, is Woods College considering a change in its mission or simply an expanded recruitment pool?

Are there opportunities at your institution to pursue your mission by becoming more diverse? If not, should your institution's mission be reexamined? What might be the advantages and disadvantages of such a reexamination?

FOREST COLLEGE

Forest is a small, residential college in the great books tradition. It would like to be more open to students from ethnic minority backgrounds, and to offer all students more options for career preparation, particularly in the sciences.

In 1985 Forest College had long prided itself on carrying forward the great books tradition. The college was small (500 students), residential, and rural (50 miles from shopping other than for necessities), and had a low student-to-faculty ratio (8 to 1). Staff and administrators also taught courses. Faculty were selected for their teaching skills and enthusiasm for round-the-clock discussion. Only half had Ph.D.'s, and perhaps only a quarter had active research interests, which they knew they would be able to pursue actively only during vacations and sabbaticals.

Alumni have expressed in many ways their satisfaction with the education they have received. Their donations (and shrewd investment advice) enabled the college to triple its endowment from the early 1970s to the mid-1980s, when it amounted to $30,000 per student. Although the college's educational program has been outside the mainstream, it has never seen this as a reason for distinguishing itself financially from other private liberal arts institutions. The combined charges for tuition, fees, room, and board amounted to $12,000 in 1985. In the 1980s a good many of its students were borrowing under the federal student loan programs and some were receiving merit-based state and institutional scholarships, but very few qualified for federal grants because at least three-quarters of the students were from upper- and upper middle-income families.

Although faculty, administration, and alumni felt little wish to change Forest's program in any fundamental way, they gave considerable thought to the relationship of a firmly anchored great books program to the tides and currents of a rapidly changing economic and social world. One impulse for considering changes in that relationship was the sheer enthusiasm of faculty and students for the educational program. If it was such an excellent program, why should others beyond its traditional clientele not have a chance to enjoy its benefits? It was troubling to the consciences of many, and awkward for all, to brag about the college and then to have to admit that its student body was virtually all White. The college enrolled a few children of Asian and Latin American ambassadors and senior business executives, but in some classes there were no Blacks at all. As one very rich and very generous trustee said, "When I tell people I am on this board, it's as if I am telling people I belong to an exclusive club—exclusive in all the bad old ways."

There was also a problem with Forest's traditional clientele. The college had long been comfortable with the assumption that any professional education its students required would be obtained by going to graduate or professional school after completing the college's program. This assumption had become less comfortable. Fewer parents, even affluent ones, were happy with the idea of offspring who would have little chance of being self-supporting without three to five years of education beyond college. The same facts of life would surely turn away many low-income and minority students if the college tried to recruit them.

Further, there was the problem of science: Many of the most intellectually agile students at Forest College loved its program, but felt they simply couldn't compete to get into prestigious graduate science programs with only the college's excellent grounding in the principles of scientific method. As a result, each college class was losing some of its most valuable intellectual leaders as they transferred to research universities in their junior year.

Some Interim Questions

Is it fair to criticize Forest on the ground that it is out of touch with economic and social trends?

Does your institution, like Forest, see diversity as a concern marginal to its traditional commitments?

Forest's president found, after a good deal of consultation with faculty, trustees, and students, that none of them wanted an across-the-board change in the college's goals, methods, or atmosphere. No one wanted to lose Forest's distinctiveness by becoming a copy of other colleges. Yet there was support, possibly even enthusiasm, for making circumscribed changes rationally related to both Forest's traditions and to its perceived problems. Recruiting minority students was seen as such a desirable change.

In the end the faculty adopted a proposal to recruit Black, Hispanic, and Asian students one by one through a program of alumni visits to high schools. It was agreed that a reasonable goal would be to recruit 10 to 20 percent of the next entering class among members of these groups. It was, however, also agreed that it would be better *not* to meet this goal than to enroll students who did not know what they were getting into or who did not seem likely to thrive at Forest.

Thus the recruiters opened themselves up to fairly wide ranging discussion of both Forest's program and the ideas the potential recruits had about what college should be like. The recruiters often returned with new perspectives. They had to deal with questions like the following:

> "How do I explain to my parents that I am going to study Aristotle rather than engineering?"

> "I intend to be a pre-med student. What medical schools do your students get into?"

"My father was a company representative in Taiwan, and I want to build on that to make a career in international trade. What can I get at Forest College that will help me?"

"I like lots of Anglos, but I just can't go someplace where there are only five Chicanos. How many would there be in my class at Forest?"

"My math is great, but I don't speak English, not really well, and I know my accent is terrible. So would I have to sit around every day talking with people running circles around me and putting me down every time I use a word wrong?"

"So students argue and discuss a lot, right? So if I have anything to say about justice, I am going to think about justice for Black people. So my examples are not going to make sense to anybody else at Forest. How can anybody there listen to *me*?"

Although it was somewhat harder to recruit ethnic minority students than the college expected, it met its goals, probably because the alumni recruiters found themselves regarded as mentors and sponsors, roles that few recruiters from large public institutions had been prepared to play. The entering class of 1986 included eight Blacks, eight Hispanics, and four Asians.

The year went well, but there was a kind of exhaustion by the following May that none of the faculty remembered experiencing before. Said one, "It was a case of always being embarrassed by things I did not know, groping for examples that wouldn't seem to come from outer space to these kids. And then seeing how embarrassed *they* were, and trying to cover for their embarrassment and my own at the same time. And this went on every day."

Financially, recruitment of the new students seemed to work out. To allow for the minority and other initiatives, it had been decided that each successive freshman class would be increased in size by 20 percent. Although many of the new students would need large aid packages, an extra 5 percent tuition increase would take care of much of the cost. The rich and embarrassed trustee enabled the college to meet additional costs by offering a $200,000 challenge gift that was fully matched by his fellow alumni. The college president (who served as the college's de facto comptroller) thought, however, that even more money would be needed.

Some Interim Questions

What might it have felt like to be one of Forest's recruiters? One of the potential recruits? One of the faculty?

Are your students, like Forest's new recruits, focused on concerns that make it hard to convey the institution's distinctive ethos?

He figured that increasing the size of formal classes from eight to 10 would provide some further capital to invest in new ventures. And he decided that now was the time to end what he considered the hopelessly inefficient practice of offering foreign languages other than Greek on a tutorial basis.

His idea was (gently) to direct the extra money and time into a computer sciences program. As he argued, "Reasoning is the heart of a great books program, and logic is the heart of computer science. If this isn't a marriage made in heaven, what is? It will certainly do very well on earth. Our graduates (and their parents) will need have no fear about their employability. Computer science will help our graduates get into graduate or professional school; if not that, to get a real job."

The president did not see the diversity effort and the computer science program as separate initiatives. He was mindful of the questions the ethnic minority students had asked when they met with the college's recruiters. With a computer science program, the recruiters would have something thoroughly modern to offer, as well as the great books, when they toured the high schools. This attraction would be meaningful for Black, White, Hispanic, and Asian students alike. Indeed, he had hopes (which might be just fantasies) that computers would provide all students a new common language. The first year with the new students showed that they certainly needed that. Then, too, Aristotle might seem less alien. Certainly, Aristotle was no more abstract or remote from the experience of many of the new students than computer science.

The college was not, however, ready to launch the computer sciences program when students returned in the fall semester of the second year of the diversity program. A third of the minority freshmen of the year before did not return. Those who did return as sophomores seemed very willing and able to help the new cohort of minority students to feel at home. This was very satisfying to the president and the faculty. An opinion that was passed around could be paraphrased like this: "The ones who came back must like the place. It is their place now, and they will be protective of it. Things are going to be fine."

This felt proprietorship of the new students had implications, however, that few of the traditional students and faculty had anticipated. If it was now "their" college, it should make room for things they enjoyed and cherished. And they felt they were making a contribution, as faculty acknowledged. Classroom discussion had a richness it had not had before. Sometimes this was because an experience related by one of the minority students made a fragment of text come alive in a new way, so that the text fairly glowed with meaning. Sometimes it was because of a kind of parallax view that made a central issue stand out in three dimensions.

Thus, the minority students felt that the college should recognize their presence. There should be discussion of the classics of Spanish moral philosophy (and an annual Latino cultural fair?). There should be a Black history section in the library (and a portrait of Martin Luther King beside all those pale, white marble busts of Greek philosophers?). There was perhaps the feeling, tinged with anger, that if the college had been more welcoming in such respects, the minority students who had dropped out would not have done so.

Some of these issues were grist for class discussion in the great books tradition, but some were not. It was a complication that second-year students, who understood the great books tradition, raised the issues, but that first-year students, who did not yet understand that tradition, tended simply to assert their demands as rights.

The president found, however, that his biggest problem was the faculty, not the students. Faculty who had felt exhausted the previous spring now found themselves facing larger classes. There were rumblings about burnout, and talk of resignations, very rare before. And salary issues were likely to be extremely difficult. Minority students were now becoming visible around the campus in more than token numbers, but the faculty was entirely Anglo with the exception of one Cuban émigré.

The president and faculty were more than willing to hire minority faculty, and the teaching orientation of the college made research specialization nothing like the problem it was at research institutions. But Forest College had a pipeline problem of its own: there had been few minority graduates of great books programs around the country in the past 20 years, and most of them were prosperous lawyers and businessmen. Forest's only hope was to bid for recent minority Ph.D.'s, and the bidding would prove expensive. Add to this the salary premium necessary to attract faculty for the computer science program, and the president faced the possibility of a faculty of which the newest members were paid much more than the dedicated majority who had committed their whole careers to the college. The president could find money for the new hires, but now he felt he must find more for the large increase in all salaries that alone would be accepted as fair.

Some Concluding Questions for Discussion

Has Forest's recruitment of ethnic minority students changed its mission? Has the computer science initiative changed Forest's mission?

What further risks and benefits do you think might flow from these two initiatives?

Are there always other institutional goals that compete with—or complement—a commitment to diversity, as at Forest?

Does a more diverse student body always have important consequences for faculty, as at Forest?

DILEMMA

University faculty discuss the relative priorities of a multicultural curriculum against one that stresses traditional liberal arts objectives.

Four professors have arrived an hour early for the first meeting of Alpha University's new Committee on the Goals and Content of the Curriculum. The time of the meeting had been changed, and none of the four had heard of the change. Professor A is at the business school, Professor B is the chair of the mathematics department, Professor C is in the history department, and Professor D is a professor of engineering.

PROFESSOR A: It's inexcusable the way this place is run. Surely, someone could have telephoned us to let us know the time had been changed.

PROFESSOR B: They could have, if departments had all the secretarial support the administrators have.

PROFESSOR C: Well, we might as well use the time. What were each of you going to say?

PROFESSOR D: Yes. Let's get the bugs out of our speeches.

PROFESSOR A: But first, let me ask why we are here. Why are we going to have this committee? For my part, I want this committee to challenge all the smugness I see around the place. I'm appalled sometimes. But I'm sure all of you have your agendas, too.

PROFESSOR B: Mine is to tighten up on priorities in undergraduate education. Too many trendy, superficial courses have got by the course approval process. But I *don't* think we are smug, just a fairly happy place, as universities go. We are all pretty comfortable, and I think that includes the students as well as the faculty.

PROFESSOR A: Strike "smug." But aren't we getting just a bit uncomfortable *about* being so comfortable? I think our students are wondering about the big, strange world out there and worrying that they are not getting much to prepare themselves for it. And that should bother us too.

PROFESSOR C: It does. It's a worry faculty always have.

PROFESSOR D: Well, we engineers have no choice. Our graduates have to know the current state of technology in their fields or they simply won't get jobs.

PROFESSOR A: That may be so, but most of us completely ignore how the world is being reshaped by technology. We produce excellent engineers, of course. But no one thinks much about the implications of technology for everyone else. For example, markets are really different, now that they are global. Every securities analyst knows what is happening in Tokyo tomorrow morning.

PROFESSOR C: Even the international dateline has become an anachronism. Tomorrow is today.

PROFESSOR A: And everything else in the international economy is changing in ways just as confusing. Capital, technology, and management skills are being redistributed, separated, and recombined in ways that give strange twists to our ideas about who does what. An American computer company has Thais assembling parts made in Singapore. Japanese managers teach production techniques to Americans from Kentucky so that they can manufacture Japanese cars in Indiana. TV sets become a commodity like soybeans.

I think our students are generally quite unaware of all this. I hope our MBAs are aware of it, but I don't feel sure even about them. Most of our students think you can still expect to get a job in a firm like the Proctor and Gamble of the 1950s or the federal bureaucracy of the 1960s or the school systems of the 1970s. We have to tell them it isn't so.

PROFESSOR B: Fine, you tell them that in the business school. I am too busy teaching them mathematics. And, I hope, the English department is too busy teaching them how to read a book and the psychology department is too busy teaching them about the mind. We have enough on our plates, and our priorities were about right, until multiculturalism and the like came on the scene.

PROFESSOR D: Which brings up something that I simply don't understand. What is the conflict over multiculturalism anyway? I guess people who become engineers just want to know how machines work, and from an early age. For us, multiculturalism is really the same: The question is how societies and cultures work.

PROFESSOR C: Yes, how they work—but also how they change. Society has changed dramatically for me, as a woman, in my professional lifetime. Students need to understand such changes. Your students need to land jobs. *All* our students need to land on their feet in a very changeable world, and that is the problem curriculum reform has to deal with.

PROFESSOR A: As things are, our students are more likely to land on somebody else's toes. They are often completely unaware of how members of other ethnic groups live. I say our students need a map. Everyone was more or less the same in their suburban high schools, but they won't be the same in the places they end up working. Whether they go into business or become engineers or health professionals, they are going to find themselves among people they will think of as having strange accents, puzzling mannerisms, more muted or more vehement ways of making a point. The chances for missed communication, conflict, inefficiency, and all the little paranoias of the workplace are staggering.

Our graduates are simply not prepared for the kinds of problem solving such workplaces will require of people. This means they are not prepared to be creative and productive in the world as it will exist. And they won't be. Their paychecks will show it.

Do we do anything at all about this? Yes, we do, but it is pretty pathetic. We take in students with a lot of naive goodwill, and by the second semester they are either tongue-tied or mildly hostile in the presence of other ethnic groups. The only students who take international economics are ones who plan to become professors or MBAs. We have a cooperative education program, but it enrolls a grand total of 50 students. We have an international education program, but it consists mostly of women planning to take a traditional junior year in Florence or Paris.

PROFESSOR C: Hold on, I can't let that remark pass about the junior year abroad. Are you aware that more of our women graduates than our men join the Peace Corps? It is we *faculty* that are isolated from the world around us.

PROFESSOR B: Well, maybe this committee is going to be less boring than most. You two are plain wrong. Aren't you assuming that our job is to prepare students for the world *as it is right now*? But aren't things going to continue to change? If we are out of date, things won't stand still while we catch up.

PROFESSOR C: True enough, but don't we have at least to try?

PROFESSOR B: Oh, I'm for *trying*. But exactly *what* should we try to do? Professor A says our students need a map. I say they need a compass.

Do the "map" and "compass" metaphors make sense to you? Are there better metaphors for how education should equip students for life in a changing and diverse society?

We can't possibly be all that specific about the world our students will live in. Things change too fast. What we *can* do is what we do in mathematics: we concentrate on timeless things. The child that learns to divide an apple into equal shares learns something about fractions that applies equally to the mass of the sun and equally for everybody. It applies in a career on Wall Street or in a career as a pharmacist, and culture, ethnic or otherwise, has nothing to do with it.

And please note, mathematics can be universal *because* it is abstract. We never hear that children should be spared the learning of fractions because it is too universal and abstract. Teachers of mathematics are spared at least *that* cross.

PROFESSOR A: Your wonderful uncluttered world of mathematics! But the social sciences and the humanities *deal* in clutter. These fields are being pressed to deal with the particulars of all kinds of societies, all kinds of ethnic groups. And rightly: if we don't deal with them, that's like saying they don't exist. We just can't talk about justice or the family in the abstract and not imply that kind of denial.

PROFESSOR B: Don't get me wrong! I'm not saying we shouldn't *understand* particulars, ethnic or otherwise. And we lose much of the richness of life if we do not value them. But when push comes to shove—and you can be sure it is coming for this committee—do we give all these particulars of multiculturalism a license to crowd out what is abstract and universal?

And another thing: You talk as though our students will stop learning once they leave here. Of course they won't stop. They will learn about their varied co-workers when they are actually working with them—and better than they possibly could here at Alpha. They will learn about real particulars, on the spot and on the job, not dubious generalizations about the Black experience or the Chicano experience.

Let's face it, what multiculturalism offers us is new stereotypes for old. There is no reason to think this helps. What good is it to substitute the stereotype of the strong Black family for the stereotype of the weak Black family, if I am to work with a particular Black man? *His* family may have been strong or weak or—like most families, including mine—strong in some respects and weak in others. What good is it to substitute the stereotype of Asians as dreamy and poetic for the stereotype of Asians as quantitative and entrepreneurial? Both may be false to the real Asian I am working with.

Aren't we much better off—aren't our students better off—if education concentrates on what is universal? Isn't it most of value to our students to learn about strength and weakness in all families and all people?

PROFESSOR C: But you learn such things through learning from particular people and their histories, including their family histories and—dare I say—from their ethnic histories.

PROFESSOR B: Maybe. But if there must be crowding, I say let the universal crowd out the particular. Students need to learn the abstractions of economics because particular economies change. They need to learn about justice because "cases and controversies" change. They need to learn how scientists think, precisely because the particular problems scientists think about change all the time. To prepare our students for the real world by teaching them about our

> *What kinds of courses do you think each of the professors might propose to the committee? Could some of their objectives be combined in practice?*

> *Do you agree that colleges should seek to impart to their students knowledge that is "universal" and enduring, as contrasted to the particulars of the "here and now"? Can we—do we—make such distinctions in constructing our curricula?*

world of here and now is to give them an education that is instantly obsolete. Bringing education up to date, and only that, is self-defeating. We don't need to bring it up to date so much as to make sure it's good enough.

Yes, our students will live their lives among a diversity of intermingling cultures, but what they need is the equipment to understand the future as well as the present and the past, what are truly the constants and what are the variables. They will then be much better prepared than if they carry around your fading snapshots of the present moment.

PROFESSOR D: Constants and variables I understand. But it seems to me you are not arguing anymore that universals are somehow antagonistic to particulars.

PROFESSOR C: Right. Universals help us understand particulars, and the other way around. You, A and B, seem far apart only because you see the task of preparing students for a multicultural world as first and mainly an issue about subject matter, about what topics should be covered in what courses.

PROFESSOR A: That's right. Courses are what we faculty have some say about.

PROFESSOR B: Yes, not that we don't duck the issues when we can.

PROFESSOR C: But this subject matter perspective leaves out what is much more important: the occasions for multicultural contacts there could be right here on the Alpha campus, and the desire to learn that those contacts can stimulate. You leave out that students learn to *care* about one another. If a student has a Black roommate or shares a laboratory bench with a Latino student or is in a study group with a student from Vietnam, those contacts are going to stimulate *both* kinds of inquiry the two of you think important. The student will want to know more about the Black experience in America, the culture of Latin America, and the odysseys of Asian-American students. He will want that kind of particular knowledge, that kind of map.

PROFESSOR A: One would like to think so.

PROFESSOR C: Well, it is my guess that he will *also* have much more motivation to understand universals of the human condition, to want a compass. He will want to know what he and these fellow students have in common as human beings, as citizens living under a government of laws, as seekers of truth, and as participants in the world economy. That is, he will be motivated in a profoundly personal way to learn particulars *and* universals.

PROFESSOR B: Maybe, if we have educated him to see the difference.

PROFESSOR C: Sure, we have our work cut out for us. My point is only that the personal contacts that stimulate concern and curiosity about people of other traditions can occur right here, and this is precisely the right place for them. The courses, the books, the scholars are right here to satisfy that concern and curiosity.

Of course, we have to make sure that these great resources really are available to both satisfy and expand these interests. That is, after all, why we really do need a curriculum committee such as this. If we do the job badly we will frustrate all that awakened concern and curiosity about one another—a terrible thing to waste, to paraphrase the slogan of the United Negro College Fund. But we should never lose sight, in debating curriculum proposals, of the kind of intellectual stimulation just being on a diverse campus can provide. Our students' daily lives here are a curriculum outline we would do well to follow.

How much attention should a college devote to increasing and building upon students' ability to care about one another? What might be the consequences for the curriculum?

Background Essay

"Diversity changes nothing essential," one faculty member might say. Another might reply, "Diversity changes everything, *especially* what is essential."

It is far easier to get agreement that diversity will affect the missions of American colleges and universities in the coming decades than to get agreement about what changes it will entail. Almost all institutions now perform their missions of teaching, research, and service with the needs and prospects of the larger society in mind, and they will aspire to do so in the future as American society becomes increasingly multiethnic and multicultural. Society needs the contribution of colleges and universities in this transition, and they know it. This knowledge is a powerful and persuasive reason for embracing diversity as part of an institution's mission.

Society needs the contribution of colleges and universities in this transition, and they know it.

Yet a college or university that seeks to understand and guide its engagement with diversity finds the task far from simple. It cannot just be a matter of accommodating more ethnic minority students, because all students will find themselves learning in new ways from new experiences. As campuses become more diverse, faculty are finding that their teaching methods are changing. Intellectually, diversity cannot just be a matter of doing research on additional topics, because focus on a greater variety of cultures will change the way we view cultures already investigated. This is already happening in the humanities and social sciences. Finally, a mission for diversity cannot just be a matter of serving additional ethnic communities off campus, because their needs and new relationships with the institution will almost certainly give rise to new concepts of service content and service delivery in the professions.

The difficulty of defining a college or university's mission in such a context of transformation is no small problem, because an institution's mission is the sense of purpose that justifies its existence and to which its energy, time, and money are devoted. It helps here to be candid about the ambigu-

Thought Experiment

A DISCOVERY IN THE ARCHIVES

The academic vice-president of College A happens to find in some old files a mission statement for the college drafted in 1950, when the college was an all-male, virtually all-White selective liberal arts college. The opening sentence of the statement reads, "The goal of College A is to educate the whole man, to prepare students for excellence in lives of scholarship and public service, and to encourage an appreciation of the life of the mind."

How would you edit this sentence to fit College A in the 1990s, still a selective liberal arts college, but now coeducational and ethnically diverse? Are there concepts (as opposed to phraseology) in the old statement that may not need to be changed?

ities in the concept of "mission." Consider four summary formulas that attempt to capture what is in our thinking when we use the term *mission*:

"Our mission is what we are."

"Our mission is how we see ourselves."

"Our mission is what we do."

"Our mission is what we want to become."

These four formulas overlap enough so that it would be possible to create a definition of mission that would incorporate elements of all four, and people commonly seem to operate in terms of such a composite definition. Yet, each formula of the four directs attention in a quite different direction when the issue is whether a college or university's mission can or should change. This could not be clearer than when the issue is the relationship of an institution's mission to ethnic diversity.

Take the formula "Our mission is what we are." It suggests that including diversity is mainly a task of making room for people and ideas of diverse origins. It suggests that any problems are likely to be ones of finding some extra space—in budgets, enrollments, and course offerings—without too much crowding. This formula underlines the "givenness" and stability of mission, a very helpful property in providing orientation—a kind of polar star—for the activities of many different people with different agendas. But this formula does not suggest that the coming of diversity is a seriously transforming process that will affect how students and faculty work together, and that will influence which intellectual endeavors are attractive.

Consider, then, the second formula, "Our mission is how we see ourselves." Whether what we see is an idealized vision or a quite matter-of-fact picture, the formula suggests the values of introspection. It directs attention inward, not outward to the new values diversity is likely to bring. This formula has the enormous value of calling for an assessment of the effectiveness of given resources and arrangements, what faculty, libraries, and computer centers actually contribute. In the interest of diversity, it suggests the vital need for a baseline appraisal, so that in getting "from here to there" we will know where "here" is. Its fault is that it promotes the assumption that the values, styles, and

Thought Experiment

A DIAGRAM EXERCISE

The mission of a college or university can be thought of as having "central" elements, which may include such things as teaching, research, training in certain skills, or imparting a world view. Other elements are more "peripheral," supporting "central" functions or increasing comfort and amenity.

1. Using a diagram of concentric circles, where would you place elements of your institution's mission?

2. How would you overlay your institution's concerns for diversity on such a diagram? Would they affect central elements? Would they include some central elements and also some peripheral elements?

Voice

"Much of the success of (our program) comes from the college community's commitment to the success of students—whatever that entails for the institution. The support for this educational mission, moreover, is truly college-wide. Trustees, regents, and alumnae as well as faculty and administration regard the education of academically underprepared students as an important part of the college's mission."

(Small college administrator)

perspectives that are already present on campus can be understood without relation to those of diversity that are not yet present. For example, what books, archives, and artifacts will best support study of Southeast Asian cultures? How might such studies change libraries?

The third formula has different virtues and different inadequacies. "Our mission is what we do" suggests the values of doing the job well, of getting priorities right for the accomplishment of the job. But it also suggests that we know what the criteria are for doing it well, for what comes first and what is secondary, for what counts as accomplishment. Diversity may turn out to call for considerable modification in each of these sets of criteria as "the job" changes. Diversity means that the job—whether research, education, or service—will be judged by new eyes that see means and ends differently. Should all students take American history? What should the syllabus be like?

An institution is very unlikely to have a clear picture of what it wants to be as a diverse community until it is well along in becoming one.

The final formula, "Our mission is what we want to become," has a quite different merit and a quite different defect. Its merit is that it underlines the elements of aspiration and resolve for the future in an institution's mission. Its defect in coming to terms with diversity is that an institution is very unlikely to have a clear picture of what it wants to be as a diverse community until it is well along in becoming one, and even that picture must, for a considerable time, be tentative and provisional. It is only with the presence and active participation of students, faculty, staff, and trustees from ethnic minority backgrounds that goals and ideas will be recast to reflect fully the potentials of diversity.

Thought Experiment

A CASE OF RECRUITMENT AND MISSION

College B has found that the most effective means of recruiting ethnic minority students is to work closely with several high schools in the area. A pattern has evolved of frequent visits back and forth between the college and the schools. Faculty, advisors, and students of both the college and the schools participate in conferences, orientation sessions, and tutoring.

1. Is College B probably changing its sense of its mission through these activities?

2. What are some things a college may learn about itself through outreach efforts? What has your institution learned in this way?

Given the inevitable uncertainties, it is hard for an institution that has undertaken to engage diversity as part of its mission to know how far its next steps will take it. There are moments of optimism and moments of discouragement as the process unfolds. It has often happened, for example, that a college or university feels it has taken the largest step when it has succeeded in recruiting a student body much more representative of the population at large. It has sought to be inclusive and now it does, indeed, include sizable numbers of ethnic minority students. It feels it has made the gift of extending opportunity to participate in its mission, often not initially realizing either what the new students have to give the college, nor how difficult it may be for them to grasp the opportunities that are there. These discoveries, when they are made, are in some ways parallel to those colleges and universities found themselves making when large numbers of veterans arrived on campus after World War II who worked harder and asked harder questions than faculty often expected.

If the new students feel unappreciated, disoriented, and disaffected on campus because the campus is unprepared for them, there can be major changes in the institution's self-perception. The college or university perceives inadequacies in itself that it was previously unaware of and recognizes the need to make new, major efforts, first to improve the participation of ethnic minority students and then to invest more of its energies in assuring that *all* students have better prospects of success. The institution that may have thought its task was to absorb the new students in its existing academic community finds that the complex relations among the new students themselves and among the new students and its traditional students assume more complex patterns. New students and traditional students may socialize separately and study together. As these changes occur, they put the institution's mission in a new light.

It can seem a troubling light, given the value of seeing an institution's mission as something given and stable. Although a mission is often seen as springing from purposes long established, even an articulation of inertia, it may help to bear in mind that the habit of viewing institutional mission in this way often contradicts actual history. The missions of almost all American colleges and universities have been shaped by the perceived needs and the perceived opportunities of the day. A liberal arts college quite often was founded to train ministers for a church, then transformed to provide common perspectives and background to an emerging managerial class, and then transformed again into a training ground for young people destined to go on to professional or graduate school. Quite often a state university started as a land-grant college, became a large-scale outreach program for the discovery of intellectual talent, and then became a research institution.

Thought Experiment

DIVERSITY AND OCCUPATIONAL PROGRAMS

College C offers a basic liberal arts curriculum but its emphasis is on widely recognized technical training programs in the health professions, accounting, and production technology. Over the last 10 years College C has increased ethnic minority enrollments in these technical fields to 30 percent of its student body. The college's standards for graduation are effectively set by licensing bodies in the various fields.

College C would like to take action to recognize that its mission now encompasses ethnic diversity, while affirming the excellence of its traditional mission of technical training. The following suggestions are made:

- Introduce multicultural content in the basic liberal arts curriculum.
- Develop student exchanges and other links with institutions in Latin America, Asia, and the Caribbean.
- Ask technical faculty to introduce ethnic-related topics, projects, and texts wherever possible.
- Develop leadership programs for professionals working in multicultural settings.

1. Would each proposal affirm College C's mission? How?
2. Which seems most useful? How would you rank the proposals?
3. Does College C face an easier or harder task than your institution in embracing diversity as part of its mission?

Each of these changes of mission was a response to a combination of needs and opportunities—the needs and opportunities of a growing, changing, and mobile country. Each successive mission demanded immense, sometimes heroic, effort: money had to be found, teachers and students recruited, standards reinvented. The ethnic diversity of the United States represents but another in the series of challenges that institutions have faced. Just as those other challenges led to new missions and new achievements, so can this one.

Why, then, is diversity so often regarded as a threat rather than a challenge or a gift? No doubt it is in part because fundamental change is almost always disconcerting. Perhaps part of the explanation is a sense of the fragility of the received missions of many institutions. Some colleges and universities may feel that their missions are at risk unless they have students with very high SAT scores and a curriculum that prepares students well for the demands of elite graduate and professional schools. Even when these institutions decide that efforts to become more diverse are desirable, even imperative, faculty tend to worry that standards may be compromised. It has literally been generations since some institutions even contemplated a revised mission, and this fact may make any change seem dangerous. In contrast, those institutions that have seen themselves all along as vehicles for mobility on the part of first-generation students often seem to be much more comfortable with increasingly diverse student bodies. These institutions find it normal to accept students as they find them and view the institution's contribution in "value-added" terms.

Those institutions that have seen themselves all along as vehicles for mobility on the part of first-generation students often seem to be much more comfortable with increasingly diverse student bodies.

In some cases a source of defensiveness about mission is a feeling that the institution's existence as a community is threatened by the separatism that often is visible as the minority members of a college or university become numerous enough to have the option of spending a good part of their time in the company of others of the same ethnicity. It is often forgotten or ignored that students have always congregated along lines of interest and identification such as social class, intellectual interest, and religion, and that within such groups there is great internal variety and many individuals with important ties outside the group.

Another reason why some see diversity as a threat to a college or university's mission consists of recent developments in the humanities and some of the social sciences that put forward the idea that different people in different circumstances grasp different and perhaps irreconcilable versions of the truth. The merits of this view to one side, it is sometimes perceived as a threat to deeply held convictions. When one faculty member sits down next to another from a different discipline in the faculty club, there has traditionally been the companionable assumption that each pursues part of the truth in his or her own way. A philosophic threat to this assumption can seem a threat to a mission framed with the common pursuit of truth in a central position. Since diversity clearly brings with it different perspectives on society and culture, it may be seen as of a piece with this threatened fracturing of truth.

When these various reasons for defensiveness in the face of diversity are made explicit, it is hard to see them as very good reasons for rejecting the positive challenges of diversity to an institution's mission.

- The process of adapting to ethnic diversity entails no attack on the academic seriousness of the best undergraduate education.

- Most people, very naturally, want to be part of *both* their supportive ethnic groups and the larger academic community.

- It is patently unfair to burden ethnic minority students in general with any intent to fragment academic communities on ideological or philosophical lines. They are not, unless they choose to be, either 1960s radicals or 1980s critical theorists.

None of the foregoing is in conflict with the fact that different institutions have different "baseline" missions subject to transformation as they engage diversity. All are challenged. A small religious college finds that it needs to distinguish elements of its instruction and practice that spring from its religious faith from those elements that spring from its previous single-ethnic culture. A research university will no doubt continue to emphasize disciplinary excellence in tenure decisions more than will a comprehensive university, but both will reexamine the kinds of meritorious research and teaching they will reward. A specialized institution that looks to a particular profession for its standards will find that much of diversity's impetus for transformation comes from a parallel transformation of the profession itself.

Perhaps the best perspective on the transformation of institutional missions that diversity will bring is gained by extrapolating from history. Colleges and universities usually can recognize themselves in what they were 50 years ago. They are often proud of what they uniquely were, but they are also proud of how their missions have evolved and would not want to go back. Fifty years from now those missions will have been transformed again by engaging ethnic diversity, and again colleges and universities will be proud of what they have become.

Voice

"There's concern because diversity and multiculturalism seem like 'relativism,' and in small, Protestant schools, truth is usually spelled with a capital T. Truth comes to us through scripture, through the history of European civilization, and through the founding fathers. It's propositional. There is natural law. What good has ever come out of the Third World? Asia? What can poor people teach us? If there is value in The Wretched of the Earth, *don't let it replace* The Federalist Papers *on our reading lists."*

(Professor at a small Protestant college)

REFERENCES AND RESOURCES

American Council on Education. *Diversity Initiatives in Higher Education.* Washington, DC: American Council on Education, 1993.

Chaffee, E. E., and Tierney, W. G. *Collegiate Culture and Leadership Strategies.* Phoenix, AZ: American Council on Education/Oryx Press, 1988.

Green, M. F., ed. *Minorities on Campus : A Handbook for Enhancing Diversity.* Washington, DC : American Council on Education, c1989.

Koepplin, L. W., and Wilson, D. A., eds. *The Future of State Universities: Issues in Teaching, Research, and Public Service.* New Brunswick, NJ: Rutgers University Press, c1985.

Lee, D. J., ed. *Ethnic Minorities and Evangelical Christian Colleges.* Lanham, MD: University Press of America, c1991.

Liberal Education 77(1) (Jan./Feb. 1991) (Special issue: "Discussing Diversity").

Liberal Education 77(3) (May/June 1991) (Special issue: "Engaging Cultural Legacies").

2

THE SOCIAL CONTEXT

CASE

ARBORVILLE STATE UNIVERSITY

A public university considers how to strengthen community and academic values in an ethnically diverse student body. The context is a debate about who should have a claim on space in a new residence hall.

The site of Arborville State University was donated 80 years ago by developers who believed a state institution would promote commercial development and would put their new community "on the map." The site of the town is attractive—a narrow shelf between sea and mountains—but this geography also has its drawbacks. Residential and commercial development has been so successful, and room for growth is so limited, that off-campus rents are among the highest in the state. The university has successfully pressed its strong case for state funding to build more housing for students. The first of the new dormitories, Franklin Hall, will be ready for occupancy next year.

It is widely accepted that the new residential facility should not be used simply to house students, but should be part of their education as well. The university's problem is to decide which students should have this opportunity of living together and what their living together should mean. There have been several proposals:

- The dean of students proposes that the dormitory house a cross section of first-year students. She argues that most of them experience similar problems of being away from home for the first time and similar academic and social needs in becoming acculturated to the university environment. Getting through their first year together could be a source of lasting and valuable bonds. If there turn out to be more applications for housing than spaces, the administration should be careful to ensure that spaces will be allocated, first, according to the percentage ethnic composition of the first-year class and, second, according to applicants' special difficulties in obtaining off-campus housing—for example, the special difficulties of disabled students. Any other system could be seen as exacerbating inequalities and the kinds of individual and group isolation these inequalities cause.

- The vice-president for academic affairs suggests that the new residence hall *not* be open to first-year students but should be an "Honors House," and open only to sophomores, juniors, and seniors. Given the likely competition for this housing, a space should be offered as a reward for demonstrated academic achievement. The vice-president is moved to make this suggestion by the constant stream of complaints he receives from faculty about the inadequate skills of students and an all-too-common lack of motivation to do anything about them. The vice-president acknowledges that there is a risk that one or two ethnic groups could be over-represented, but he insists that some measure of academic achievement could be devised that would result in approximate ethnic proportionality.

- The chair of the Ethnic Studies Department urges that the university take this opportunity to establish ethnic-theme housing, with a floor or two of the new building allocated to students from a particular non-White ethnic background and other students who would like to experience life in another ethnic milieu and to learn from student-organized programs in the group's culture. She argues that unless living arrangements along these lines are available, too many students will get the idea that ethnic cultures are to be observed and analyzed rather than fully lived.

- The director of the Office of International Student Affairs urges that the new dormitory be an "International House," offering a welcoming home base for students from other countries and an experience of cosmopolitan living for American-born students. The director notes that foreign students often have excruciating housing problems. He is not known for having much influence in university affairs, but hopes to gain support from the president, who has often expressed concern about students' parochialism and lack of preparation for life in the "Global Village."

- The School of Engineering has a more modest proposal than any of the others. It wants to stake a claim to one floor of Franklin Hall to house participants in its junior year "Project Innovation" program, in which students in collaborative teams mentored by faculty compete in inventing a device or process. The program encourages students to draw on several specializations, develop collaborative skills, and stretch their minds. The camaraderie of living as well as working together would give a further boost to this program that already has achieved a national reputation. The teams have usually been multiethnic in composition, and the school offers to guarantee that they will all be so in the future.

- A final proposal, developed by a group of faculty members, has been publicized in the student newspaper. It calls for a "Democracy House," whose contribution would be an experience of self-government. Residents would have the responsibility of developing their own constitution, laws, and courts. They would not, however, have any say about which students are allocated spaces in the resident hall. Allocation would be made using a formula that achieved an ethnic, gender, and socioeconomic distribution as close to that of the nation as a whole as possible. The residence hall community would have to deal with its members as it finds them, each with his or her own special talents and needs.

Residents would have to find their own ways of accommodating both "nerds" and "social" students, political activists and private careerists, very bright individuals and fairly dull ones. They would have to build their own structure of democratic accommodation.

The president was intrigued by this set of proposals for two reasons. First, she found it striking that none of them would require a change in the name of the residence hall. Each of them had some connection with the career or interests of Benjamin Franklin. She could easily draft in her mind the dedicatory speech she could give at the opening of the new facility, in each case making the Franklin connection.

Second, she was struck by the extent to which each of the proposals brought the outside world on campus. Each in some way was an attempt to take into account the kind of society the students lived in, both its opportunities and its unresolved problems. The contribution of the university was to help overcome the problems and build on the opportunities. As a community it had both to reflect the broader society and to be better than it was—to be more rational, creative, and sensitive. She could put that in her speech, too.

The provost agreed with all this, but the varied proposals also brought out his habits of political pragmatism. Weren't there ways in which two or more of these proposals could be combined so that more than one objective could be achieved and more than one constituency would be happy with the result?

How would you respond to the provost's question? What objectives could be combined? Are all of the objectives equally consistent with accomplishing goals of ethnic diversity?

If combining objectives would not be feasible, how would you rank the objectives of all the proposals from the point of view of society's interests? From the point of view of campus community?

What issues on your campus have their origins in issues, problems, and opportunities of the larger society? How do they link up with ethnic diversity?

DILEMMA

OMICRON UNIVERSITY

A campus task force discusses problems of verbal abuse and free speech and their connection with tensions in the larger society.

THE GENERAL COUNSEL: The president has asked me to bring all of us together to talk about how we can prevent incidents of abusive speech on campus. He asked *me* to convene the group precisely because, being a lawyer, I can perhaps put the legal issues "on hold" while we think about what we really *ought* to do about abusive speech as an academic community and what speech we really *ought* to protect. Only then will we be in a position to consider our legal posture.

Is it really possible for a college or university to develop policies on abusive speech and academic freedom without dealing with First Amendment legal issues?

THE CHAIR OF WOMEN'S STUDIES: I guess I can accept that, but only with reservations. Our problems with abusive speech come right out of our history as a society of oppression and conflict, and we have constitutional rules for handling those things. We shouldn't kid ourselves that we can ever escape either the social conflict or the rules. We are not Shangri-la.

THE HEAD OF STUDENT HOUSING: No one is saying that we are. But some of the abuse we have seen is strictly homegrown. Take the lyrics of that photocopied fraternity song that came to light. The tune was "Onward Christian Soldiers," but almost every line used some really nasty ethnic or sexist epithet. You know what their defense was? That they needed the epithets for the rhyming scheme! The fact is they were abusing people for *fun*. It was college student cruelty pure and simple, not something they got from their parents or anywhere else.

THE EDITOR OF THE STUDENT NEWSPAPER: That one was a hard call for us. We ended up opposing disciplinary sanctions. After all, if you are in the newspaper business, print is print, and print is sacred, even photocopies. But we also decided not to reprint the lyrics. We didn't feel we had to *join* in the abuse.

THE DEAN OF STUDENT SERVICES: And I think you were being responsible. But did the legal formulas, like "fighting words" help much in reaching your decision? I doubt it. People get entangled in those formulas, and when they do, the pain and humiliation abused people feel gets side-tracked.

THE ASSOCIATE PROVOST: And anyway, the formulas don't tell us anything about the phenomenon. What do we know, really, about how serious the problem is and whether it is getting worse? As a woman and a Jew, I shuddered when I read those lyrics, but as a scientist I need to understand. The abuse was cruel, homegrown or not. Where does it come from and how much of it is there?

THE GENERAL COUNSEL: If you mean, what do we know about the frequency of things like racial epithets and sexist jokes and whether the frequency is increasing, I don't know how you could ever find out.

THE DIRECTOR OF INSTITUTIONAL RESEARCH: Hold on, I think there are some things we *do* know. I think we really do know that the frequency of contacts between members of different groups has necessarily increased, simply because the student body is now much more ethnically mixed. The salad used to be white iceberg lettuce. We now have a full salad bar. There are more chances of contact, therefore there are more chances of injury, even if students are no more ill-disposed toward one another than they have been in the past.

Who are some other people who should be represented in a meeting such as this?

THE DEAN: That's right. And let's not forget that those contacts are also chances for good-natured talk, for understanding one another, liking one another. We must not "chill" *that* kind of speech.

THE CHAIR: I agree, but I think it is a mistake to concentrate our attention just on what happens on campus. This is the place where we have the responsibility, of course, and we have an obligation to do what we can. But, fundamentally, we are *not* talking about a campus problem, but the result of what has happened and is happening throughout the society.

THE HEAD OF STUDENT HOUSING: Like what?

THE CHAIR: Well, for example, it is often claimed that women and members of minority groups are "oversensitive," and they are blamed for this. Surely not. It's just that our society has come far enough in overcoming sexism and racism that the recipients of abuse have decided that they just "don't have to take it anymore." I very much doubt that sensitivity is greater. Rather, acceptance of injury is less—it is less expected, less "normal," less inevitable.

THE DIRECTOR: I suspect that you are right, but I also suspect that there are qualitative changes, too, and again these come from the larger society. Social mobility leaves its scar tissue. Most of the Black, Latino, and Asian students on campus have fought hard to get here, and their parents have fought and sacrificed to make it possible for their children to go to college. These students are not about to let these achievements be demeaned.

THE DEAN: And let's not forget *downward* mobility either. You remember the case of that White engineering student who defaced the poster for a reggae concert with racist editing? I had sources for looking into that case, because the student was from a local high school and his father had done some construction work for some friends of ours. It turned out that the student was only able to go to college because of money from his grandmother. His own father is unemployed at least half the time. But the son had good high school grades in math, so he got into the university. Then he finds Asian students out-scoring him on every test.

THE EDITOR: So he takes it out on *Blacks*?

THE DEAN: Exactly. The social and economic insecurity in a family like that is tremendous. In the old, old way, fear and hostility toward the world at large is channeled into abuse toward the group that is most vulnerable, most "different." As so often, that means us African Americans.

THE CHAIR: Yes. Students come here and bring with them intact all the hurt, envy, and fear of the outside world. That is sad but inescapable.

THE DIRECTOR: Yes, it is sad. But I think I see a strategic opening even here. Isn't it as though students are seeking out confirmation for the prejudices they bring, or confirmation of their expectations of prejudice in others? There is a kind of perverse experimentalism in some of these incidents of racial and gender tension. What we have to do is offer opportunities for the opposite kind of experiment—experiments in getting to know one another, really talking to one another, being rational, being mutually supportive. We should see our task as an institution as one of bringing that experimental stance over to the side of multicultural understanding. We may need a speech code to prevent abusive speech, but the speech code that I would have the greatest hope for is one that *requires* students to speak out, to say what they think, to talk their way through feelings of fear and envy.

THE ASSOCIATE PROVOST: I'm for that.

THE GENERAL COUNSEL: I agree, too, but we still have to think about protecting people. I think the president wants this group to stay with the premise that we don't want people at this university to beat up on one another, verbally or otherwise.

THE ASSOCIATE PROVOST: Of course not. But we have to draw a line between "beating up" people and saying things they would just rather not hear. For example, a university *has* to be a place where a geneticist can talk about the heritability of intelligence among ethnic groups with the fullest protection of the institution, even though, for historical reasons, most such talk is repellent to practically everybody.

THE DEAN: You make it sound easy, but is it? What if there is a nasty group of undergraduates on campus that we *know* wants to "beat up" verbally on minority students. Suppose this group publishes a flyer purporting to prove most minority students here are not capable of serious academic work and get by only by being members of "protected groups." The intention to "beat up" is there, and so is the result. But how do you distinguish this case from the geneticist's?

THE ASSOCIATE PROVOST: You don't. If these nasty kids are saying these things, they are giving us precisely the leverage we need to deal with them intellectually rather than punitively. Whatever their intentions, they are saying these things as *propositions*, and propositions can be debated and refuted. Go after them with evidence, not sanctions.

THE DEAN: You say that even though the hurt is greater and more personal? Remember, these are not tenured middle-aged professors whose theories of the tsetse fly life cycle have been challenged in a learned paper. These are first-year, first-generation college students who are having to deal with terrible self-doubt every day. Don't add to it!

THE ASSOCIATE PROVOST: I know. And let me say that I know as a woman scientist knows. Women have been told for hundreds—thousands—of years that we are unfit for science. It hurts. And brilliant women biochemists have become dietitians. We now know we have to fight back, to prove them wrong, to support one another. That's the only way. If we silence the chauvinists, there won't be the free dissent science must have.

Should an institution have policies to alleviate the pain and suffering caused by abusive speech even if such speech is protected on grounds of academic freedom or the First Amendment?

THE GENERAL COUNSEL: Let me see if I understand what you are saying by reformulating it—not, please note, as a legal rule. Are you saying that if someone utters a proposition, or implies a proposition, no matter how offensive its content—or how intentionally offensive—that speech should be protected from any sanction except for counterevidence and argument? However, if someone says something *intentionally* offensive that does *not* contain a proposition, there can be sanctions?

THE ASSOCIATE PROVOST: Yes, I think that's about it. Protect people who have something to say, even things that are pretty stupid. Protect everyone *from* people who *only* want to do harm.

THE DEAN: So if a drunken undergraduate reels off a string of racial epithets we should be able to do something about it?

THE CHAIR: That's right. It would be hard to find a proposition in such a performance. What comes out of his mouth is merely abuse, just as if he threw a beer bottle through a dorm window.

THE EDITOR: But hold on. This "proposition" test won't always work. We ran a cartoon last week making fun of the effort by the vegetarians and the environmentalists to ban hamburgers from the cafeteria. The cartoon didn't say anything you could call a proposition. It just made the ban seem ridiculous. And we certainly *meant* to offend. Does that mean we can be disciplined? I don't like the sound of that. The rest of the world is taking sides about the rain forest, jobs, and pollution. Ridicule is one of the weapons. Aren't we allowed to use it in the same way any off-campus newspaper could?

THE DEAN: Of course the cartoon is all right. Surely no one could feel personally injured, and that is what makes it different from a racist cartoon.

THE EDITOR: Well, then, take another case. There was this fraternity at Kappa College that held a South-of-the-Border party. OK, so the party *could* have been in perfectly good taste, with good Latin music and fireworks. But a couple of the fraternity members came to the party wearing white pajamas, and a couple others did a skit making fun of illegal immigration. The roof fell in. The whole fraternity was banned. Can that have been right, just because they weren't asserting any proposition and the ridicule was of an ethnic group?

THE GENERAL COUNSEL: But was there an intent to offend?

THE EDITOR: Probably not. Maybe on the part of a few. The group responsibility issue complicates the case.

THE DIRECTOR: That's just it. No rule can enable us to escape evaluation of the details of particular cases. All the same, I get a good deal of comfort from the provost's suggestion as far as it goes. We don't want to come down hard with no other reason than that someone claims to be offended. There has to be an intent to offend, and there has to be also an absence of a proposition that can be dealt with by refutation rather than disciplinary action. That criterion protects most kinds of deserving academic discourse I can think of. Sure, it does not take care of ridicule, because ridicule often does not lend itself to straightforward refutation.

THE GENERAL COUNSEL: But maybe the criterion helps somewhat, even with ridicule, because it puts the problem in a certain kind of perspective. Take the editor's case of the anti-vegetarian cartoon. The cartoon did not say that vegetarian propositions are wrong, so it cannot be refuted, strictly speaking. But it *did* say that the whole argument about the hamburgers has been overblown. The cartoon was intended to deflate the importance of the whole topic of hamburgers, implicitly asserting that there are more important things to be concerned about. And that *is* a proposition, which vegetarians and environmentalists can take on with some prospect of closure. The cartoon says something about relative values, just as do many of the political cartoons we wouldn't want excluded from regular newspapers. I take it that if your nasty student group made fun of "political correctness" in its flyer, it would merit protection on these grounds, however malicious. There could be argument on the merits, even if there could be no refutation strictly speaking.

> Is abusive speech specifically a campus problem or only part of a society-wide problem?

THE EDITOR: So humor is saved.

THE CHAIR: Some humor—perhaps most humor that is not so gratuitous as to be completely unfunny to civilized people.

THE HEAD OF STUDENT HOUSING: Civilized! Isn't that the point? Hurting people, not incidentally to something else constructive, but just for the meanness of it, is something we have to be able to deal with. And in those cases surely we are right to take the vulnerability of particular groups into account.

THE GENERAL COUNSEL: Yes, it goes to the degree of cruelty in the intention. There are in our society—probably in all societies—some people who just haven't learned or find it easy to forget how words can wound—or don't care. Some of them get into college, including this college. We have to say to them, "Look, this is a community that has offered to include you. If you haven't learned yet what it is to care about the other people in your community, or that membership entails such caring, we are going to remind you, and pretty emphatically. We won't let you destroy our community with impunity." It is not that we put limits on academic freedom. We will protect dissent because that is part of what our community is about. What we will not protect is behavior—including speech—that in no way contributes to that community.

How can a college or university use an incident of abusive speech to gain wider and deeper understanding of the institution's fundamental purposes?

THE DEAN: You should be the president's speech writer. But can you be his lawyer and turn that speech into rules the Supreme Court will pass?

BACKGROUND ESSAY

In initiating change, colleges and universities are sometimes the locomotive of society, sometimes the caboose.

The relationships between institutions of higher education and the larger society of which they are a part are so various and so complicated that no one model fits adequately, including this metaphor of a train. Some colleges and universities, such as research universities and liberal arts colleges in rural settings, are like protected enclaves, even fortresses. Other colleges and universities, especially urban commuter institutions with many older and part-time students, are responsive participants in the everyday social, economic, and political life of the society. Still, there is value in considering the train metaphor—how it is that colleges and universities have both led and followed the imperatives of the larger society related to ethnic diversity.

For much of our national history, colleges and universities were content to follow accepted norms of racial separation, and their performance was neither much better nor much shamefully worse than that of other institutions. Their students, however, had the honor of providing much of the leadership of the civil rights revolution. In the 1960s and 1970s, without waiting for court orders, many colleges and universities took the lead in seeking more ethnically diverse student bodies. In the 1980s, however, the leadership faltered and the equal opportunity initiatives—active recruitment of ethnic minorities, as students, faculty, and staff; a vast expansion of student aid; and even affirmative action—appeared to stall.

> **Voice**
>
> "Today's colleges serve a more diverse set of students than ever before, a trend likely to increase in the future. The presence of so many different racial, ethnic, age, income, and experienced groups promises much vitality; it also means that very little can be taken for granted."
>
> *(A college association report)*

Now sheer demography has become the powerful locomotive. The larger society is rapidly and visibly becoming multiethnic, so much so that even the terms "majority" and "minority" have come into question in several parts of the country. Unless the educational system becomes more effective as an avenue of advancement for mem-

Thought Experiment

PAST AND PRESENT

1. How did your own parents and grandparents enter the mainstream of American economic and social life?

2. Can you imagine members of the minority ethnic groups of today achieving participation in the same way?

3. What was the role of education in the lives of your parents and grandparents? What was the role of higher education specifically?

bers of all the groups in a multiethnic, multicultural society, there is likely to be on the one hand a great waste of needed talent and on the other a breakup of the society into mutually envious and mutually hostile ethnic groups. Both effects will hamper economic growth and competitiveness vis-à-vis other countries.

College-entry rates for most ethnic minority groups still are lower than those for Whites, and college graduation and graduate degree rates remain even more disparate. Some parts of the problem are not the regular responsibility of institutions of higher education but rather of families, schools, and other community institutions. However, even this division of labor needs reexamination, given the great success of some college and university outreach programs.

Although colleges and universities have in the last decade usually seemed to follow rather than lead, there are now abundant voices, from inside and outside the academy, asking that colleges and universities lead again. This is in part because many of the skills needed for the economy to prosper are the high-level skills that the society traditionally expects institutions of higher education to provide. But in part it is because colleges and universities have been traditionally the centers of the most reflective intercultural contact and study in our society. Their own students and faculty now expect these institutions to build on this tradition of cosmopolitanism to achieve new levels of understanding of the values, history, and unique cultural creations of the ethnic groups making up the American mosaic.

Such a renewal of higher education's leadership role is, however, controversial even within the academy. Much of the controversy springs from claims that multi–culturalism entails the assertion of group rights as distinct from the mutual respect and understanding of individuals for one another's cultures.

Voice

(In reference to service workers) ". . . those could be my parents or those people could be my family and I wouldn't want anyone to treat them badly and I want them . . . to have hope in us, that we're Hispanic, but we're not going to be the kind that are going to be snobs, that are going to run away from being Hispanic. I want them to know that I'm not going to forget who I am, where I came from. So, I speak to them in Spanish a lot of times because I want them to know that I'm still Mexican, even though I'm here."

(Chicano student)

Thought Experiment

ATTRITION AND ETHNICITY

University D has become concerned that Black and Hispanic students have a higher attrition rate than White students. The dean of students takes the lead in devising a program to address this concern, but asks the following units to make a contribution as well: the School of Business Administration, the Career Counseling and Placement Office, the Alumni Relations Office, and the Ethnic Student Center.

1. In what ways might the Dean think that these other units could contribute? Is she probably right?

2. Are there other units also important to draw into the effort?

This claim is made both by some advocates for ethnic diversity initiatives and also by some of their opponents. The advocates sometimes assert that only recognition of group rights will prevent the subordination and devaluation of the traditions of a minority group's members. The opponents assert the traditional individualism of higher education, insisting on recognition only of individual potential and achievement measured in ways that do not take account of ethnic identification.

Leadership in finding ways to resolve the controversy between group rights and individualism would be no small part of a renewed higher education leadership in building a more successful multiethnic society. Throughout the society, members of groups historically excluded from full participation demand recognition of what their exclusion has done to them as groups, over and above rights to go forward with their lives as juridically equal individuals. They wish to leave behind the vestiges of discrimination and yet to carry forward their group identifications. These demands are not contradictory, but they are obviously not easy to meet. They are not realistically met by counterdemands that members of minority groups simply shed their ethnic identity like outgrown clothes. A successfully diverse society will require accepting a continuation of group differences as both inevitable and full of promise. To lead such a society, higher education will need to devise new terms for inclusiveness and provide the means for both individual opportunity and assertions of group identity.

Colleges and universities have been traditionally the centers of the most reflective intercultural contact and study in our society.

The wider society can be expected to follow and support such leadership. Corporate America is already confronting the need for such skills and sensitivities, and this tells us much about the pragmatic side of diversity issues. Many corporate policies and practices for managing diversity emphasize dealing with the special needs of particular groups while seeking approaches that contribute to everyone's success and to overall productivity. This approach to managing diversity depends upon getting people to work together toward goals upon which individual and collective success depend. Accommodating diversity by sacrificing quality or productivity is not an acceptable option.

Thought Experiment

TOWN AND GOWN

College E is located in a suburban area 20 miles from the central city. The college has recently increased its recruitment of African-American students to 10 percent of its first-year class. There have been reports that storekeepers in the business district of the suburb sometimes put up a "closed" sign just when African-American men students approach. African-American women students say the stores don't stock the right cosmetics. Both men and women students say they are made to feel self-conscious when boarding buses or having a picnic in the municipal park.

1. Do ethnic minority students at your institution have similar problems of off-campus discrimination?

2. How might your institution approach business associations, churches, and local government about such problems?

3. Should your institution consider being more self-sufficient, so that students will have fewer occasions to go off campus? What are the pros and cons?

The society in general may not care much about the more abstruse issues that academics sometimes connect with diversity, or about the extreme sensitivity of some professors and students to particular words and phrases, but the society cares very much about how its members will be enabled to live and work together. There is nothing new in higher education's accepting responsibilities here. Preparing students for the worlds of work and civic participation have long been accepted responsibilities of American colleges and universities. Most college and university mission statements give some explicit emphasis to the importance of higher education in equipping students for the responsibilities of life after graduation. To succeed in this goal, colleges and universities must connect the learning students do with the world they will live in. This is an important part of educational quality that society will respect, for it is hard to imagine the twenty-first century as a workable enterprise for the United States without colleges and universities imparting the necessary skills and sensitivities for living successfully amid ethnic diversity.

> *Higher education will need to devise new terms for inclusiveness and provide the means for both individual opportunity and assertions of group identity.*

These challenges of diversity will not be met without fresh faculty, administration, and trustee commitment and leadership. In particular, these challenges will not be met by treating diversity as a "train on its own track"—as a set of issues that can be compartmentalized and contained apart from the central responsibility of institutional leaders, including faculty.

Colleges and universities are, of course, already engaged in developing such leadership, and with a sense of urgency. Necessarily, there is a good deal of trial and error in these efforts and much controversy, as one would expect of institutions of higher education. Criticism, constructive or not, tends to focus on matters like special admissions and self-segregation on campus that represent problems, possibly serious problems, for diversity efforts. But—it is worth asking—what if there were *no effort at all* beyond, say, meeting federal anti-discrimination requirements? The society would have to conduct its future affairs with only tiny numbers of African

> *Preparing students for the worlds of work and civic participation have long been accepted responsibilities of American colleges and universities.*

Americans and Hispanic Americans in influential positions in the professions, government, and business. Relationships of all kinds would be conducted on the basis of "us" and "them"—a misunderstood "us" and a misunderstood "them." The already growing distance between social classes might well harden into a full-blown caste system. Knowledge or wisdom (or both) would often be absent where they are most needed. It would not be a peaceful, prosperous future. The United States would be a perpetually rancorous nation, far more rancorous than anything Americans have experienced since the Civil War. To make a halfhearted effort with respect to diversity could well be catastrophic.

REFERENCES AND RESOURCES

Choy, S. P., and Gifford, A. G. *Profile of Undergraduates in American Postsecondary Institutions.* Washington, DC: U.S. Department of Education (Office of Educational Research and Improvement, National Center for Education Statistics), September 1990.

Hillabrant, W., et al. "Native American Education at a Turning Point: Current Demographics and Trends." In *Indian Nations at Risk Task Force Commissioned Papers.* Washington, DC: U.S. Department of Education (Indian Nations at Risk Task Force), 1991. ED 343 756.

Hodgkinson, H. L. *All One System: Demographics of Education: Kindergarten through Graduate School.* Washington, DC: The Institute for Educational Leadership, 1985. ED 261 101.

Hsia, J. *Asian Americans in Higher Education and at Work.* Hillsdale, NJ: Lawrence Erlbaum Assoc., 1988.

Johnston, W. B. "Global Work Force 2000: The New World Labor Market." *Harvard Business Review* 69(2) (Mar./Apr. 1991): 115+.

Jones, E. P. "The Impact of Economic, Political, and Social Factors on Recent Overt Black/White Racial Conflict in Higher Education in the United States." *Journal of Negro Education* 60(4) (Fall 1991): 524–37.

Koretz, D. M. *Trends in the Postsecondary Enrollment of Minorities.* Santa Monica, CA: Rand Corp., [1990].

Levine, A. *Shaping Higher Education's Future: Demographic Realities and Opportunities.* San Francisco, CA: Jossey-Bass, 1989.

Mortenson, T. G. *Equity of Higher Educational Opportunity for Women, Black, Hispanic, and Low Income Students.* Iowa City, IA : American College Testing Service, 1991.

The Road to College: Educational Progress by Race and Ethnicity. Boulder, CO: Western Interstate Commission for Higher Education, 1991.

Solmon, L. C., and Wingard, T. L. "The Changing Demographics: Problems and Opportunities." In *The Racial Crisis in American Higher Education,* edited by Philip G. Altbach and Kofi Lomotey, 19–42. Albany, NY: State University of New York Press, c1991.

Takaki, R. *A Different Mirror: A History of Multicultural America.* Boston, MA: Little, Brown, 1993.

Workforce 2000, Work and Workers for the 21st Century. Indianapolis, IN: The Hudson Institute, 1987.

3

DIVERSITY AND QUALITY

CASE

ORCHARD UNIVERSITY

When a professor in the business school writes a journal of a typical day in his life, he finds himself touching on ways in which ethnic diversity has changed teaching, intellectual perspectives, and extracurricular activities.

NOVEMBER 4: I am one of a group of 20 randomly chosen professors who have been asked to document in a journal that they are occupied with the educational concerns of the university, not just when in class, but much of the rest of the day as well. The idea is to prove to the legislature that we are not the drones they think we are. Of course, I think about lots of things during the day that have little to do with the affairs of the university, but I will try conscientiously to list those that do.

NOVEMBER 5, 8:00 A.M.: I am up and dressed and having breakfast. I switch the radio from my usual classical music station, which is playing the same version of the Pachelbel canon for the 15th time this week. I get the student-run station, and they are playing, of all things, the Missa Luba. I had thought that students would only listen to rock and rap, but obviously those who run the radio station think they have, or can have, much wider horizons. I guess if our newfound multiculturalism can gain a hearing for music like this, it can't be all bad.

8:45 A.M.: I am dawdling in the courtyard over a last cup of coffee before going into my nine o'clock class, and I look over the bulletin board. There are announcements for the extraordinary variety of lectures, advocacy meetings, special interest clubs, cultural events, etc., that students are offered here. Five years ago there would have been almost as many, but you could have classified most of them as announcing "fun" happenings, the meetings of crank groups, or apologetic and unconvincing attempts to make some boring event sound exciting. That isn't so now. The "fun," crank, and boring events are still there, but there are many more announcements of lectures about happenings in remote parts of the world, visits of cultural heroes, new music, and opportunities for firsthand experiences of non-White cultures. This is new. A lot of these events obviously have political axes to grind, but, even so, I find myself wondering whether I would not actually like to go to some of these things. Part of it is that the students who write the copy for the announcements seem to have a new confidence that these are things worth knowing about.

In this case, diversity is implicitly given the credit for improving various aspects of the quality of Orchard University. Are these attributions convincing?

9:05 A.M.: My class in strategic planning. This year it has been a breeze because of the way the case studies have fallen into place. I usually pound away on one theme: Without a product niche, you are dead. I *need* to pound away because your usual White business students think this is just an advanced course in marketing. But I have some Asian students this year, so I tried out a new first case study: Should a Chinese restaurant owner in a small town open up a specialty grocery store as well? The Asian students were arguing like mad from day one, and the discussion pulled everyone else in with practically no effort on my part. This included the Black students who think they know all about niche products because they have heard of fortunes made in black cosmetics.

Then we had a case that turned out to be trickier than I realized it would be: should a North American manufacturer of pharmaceuticals expand its plant in Guatemala? The niche issues got involved with some ethical questions, such as should the company advertise one of its products as like—or unlike—some terrible, useless drug that people down there have had faith in for generations? The Hispanic students weren't going to let the company get away with a thing, either way.

> To what aspects of your institution's quality has diversity made a contribution?

I am doing one thing that is a little sneaky with this class. I try to get arguments going about the appropriate math for the cases. I want the students to see the math as a common language. I think maybe I am succeeding.

10:30 A.M.: Schmoozing around at the department office, opening my mail, talking with the secretary and some T.A.'s that dropped by. They want my advice about teaching financial management. They tell me it is like teaching plumbing. I tell them it *should be* like teaching Mozart, starting with a sweet small ethnic business theme, then becoming a big corporation theme, then showing how everything comes out even in the end (just like Mozart), with dollars, marks, yen, and francs all adding up.

Noon: My daily appearance at the faculty club for lunch. The little group at my table is mixed, not just ethnically. The conversation is about whether students are smarter or dumber than five years ago and whether they are better or less well prepared. X from the psychology department says that, either way, we need to give more thought to the sequencing of courses, probably in lots of fields, certainly in his. He says we ought to think much more about what an introductory course should do, not just in content but in conveying how people in the disciplines tackle their characteristic problems, with lots of hooks to engage students. I say amen. He says there probably always have been a dozen different learning styles in a typical class and that ethnic variety has only jolted us into recognizing them. I say amen to that too.

1:30 P.M.: I had too much lunch, but I keep my appointment with my research partner anyway. She is an economic historian, and we are going to write a joint article—maybe a book—about how Japanese immigrants worked their way into the business establishment of Brazil. All kinds of parallels and contrasts with economic integration in the U.S. and elsewhere! But she and I could use a third partner, a cultural anthropologist.

3:00 P.M.: Good meeting. Now I feel I deserve a swim at the pool. The legislature will not be interested.

4:15 P.M.: Meeting of the Committee on the Case Study Method—a *very* important committee in a business school. We have a real problem. Sometimes we let students form their own teams to work on class projects, and when we do they usually turn out to be single-ethnic groups. Then sometimes we assign students to teams. Usually when we do this we make sure that the teams represent an ethnic mixture.

The trouble is that the mixed ethnic teams tend to turn in a less-finished project and get lower grades accordingly. This phenomenon has the result that both students and faculty become biased against mixed teams.

This is all wrong! The reason the mixed-team projects are not as polished is almost certainly because these teams take more time to settle down and find ways of working together. That means they have effectively less time to produce a high-quality project. I urge the committee to consider this. Here we have students doing an extremely important kind of learning—how to collaborate in a multicultural world—yet we *penalize* it! I think I may have persuaded some of my colleagues not to abandon mixed teams, but rather to allow more time for mixed-group projects. If it turns out that I have not persuaded them, I am going to ask some of the Big Chiefs on our advisory board to write strong letters saying how invaluable the mixed-team experience will be for careers in corporate America. Getting them to do so would certainly be a journal entry on the day I do it.

What problems does your institution need to solve for diversity to link up better with its quality goals?

DILEMMA

SIGMA UNIVERSITY

A committee of trustees debates how diversity and quality issues are seen by external constituencies. The context is planning for a fund-raising campaign.

The scene is the coffee shop at the hotel where the trustees of Sigma University will be meeting in the late afternoon. Several of the trustees who are members of the committee charged with planning Sigma's $100 million capital campaign join one another for breakfast before their 9:00 A.M. committee meeting.

TRUSTEE JONES: Well, we know what all of us have in common. Each of us is expected to make a pretty substantial personal gift.

TRUSTEE SMITH: That's fine with me. I still love Sigma. But it's not going to be as easy as it was in the last campaign to work up the kind of infectious enthusiasm that gets others to give. And unenthusiastic gifts are likely to be small gifts.

TRUSTEE DOE: Where did your enthusiasm go?

TRUSTEE SMITH: Well, the fact is Sigma is not the same place. And I *do* mean the racial thing. I am glad that Sigma is no longer lily-White. I would be pretty uncomfortable if it were. But we are not meeting the competition. During my first term as a trustee, we were getting more cutting-edge programs, more buildings, more endowed chairs. And it seemed to be paying off. We were getting better and better applicants. But now test scores are all over the place, and we all know that low-income kids, including minorities, are bringing the averages down. The alumni we are going to ask for contributions know it too, and every alumni publication reminds them. They see all the black and brown faces in the pictures, and they literally can't recognize their old university. It's beginning to look like the community college down the street. I think we are on thin ice.

TRUSTEE DOE: I hope you are wrong about that, and I think you probably are. The alumni that give are not doing it just out of nostalgia or wanting to compete with Stanford or USC. They know that the minority students are a terrific investment for the country, and they are glad that Sigma is doing its part. It doesn't bother them to see all the black and brown faces, or to read of the minority faculty appointments either. It shows that America is gaining the momentum to become the kind of society Sigma taught them to believe in, that Sigma wanted to be a part of.

Trustee Smith: And I'm glad for that. But I still think we have a problem. A lot of our donors want to see things getting measurably and conspicuously better. They want to hear about rising SAT scores. They want to see an exciting new science building. Those are things they recognize as quality. Sure, they want society to solve its problems of conflict and unequal opportunity. But a lot of them feel we should let public institutions do that with our tax dollars or the few private institutions so rich that our $100 million campaign is almost beneath their notice. Our alumni want to feel that their gifts to Sigma will go toward some goal of special excellence. It won't cut much ice with them to say half of the capital campaign will be for additional student-aid funds to support a lot of kids who won't very often test like geniuses, even if some of them turn out to be.

Trustee Doe: How else are we going to maintain enrollments? We want super-smart kids, courageous kids, interesting kids. Diversity, along with student financial aid, is the only way to get them. And diversity is giving us plenty of things we can point out to alumni. There are the outstanding faculty—minority and Anglo—we could not have recruited if we had not been committed to diversity. We can remind the prospects

Are the Sigma trustees really worrying about quality or only about perceptions of quality?

of the path-breaking research in public health that multiethnic team did. We can give prospective donors a chance to sit in on a class in the new American Society course. I did, and the students were far more involved in the complexities of the issues than in any course I remember from my undergraduate days. Also, it wouldn't be a bad idea to send out a good many free tickets to our theater series. That's another way alumni can see what diversity is doing for Sigma. In other words, if we convey the kind of intellectual life that diversity alone has made possible at Sigma, the SAT business will be put in perspective.

Trustee Jones: You may be right. You mention the American Society course. I sat in when they were discussing *The Federalist*. You remember how they used to do it against the backdrop of English and American colonial history? They still do, but they also talk about the use and abuse of police powers in a ghetto or barrio, and what the communist regimes of Eastern Europe got wrong in their quest for Utopia. It was terrific, and it was because of the much more diverse and international student body we now have.

Trustee Doe: That's how it struck me. But we need to find ways to monitor the results of diversity, so that we can offer more than our personal impressions as evidence of quality improvements. Has anyone talked to the institutional research office about getting the evidence?

Trustee Smith: Even with data it is still going to be a hard sell. Big gifts are only going to come in if we back them up with some very realistic long-range plans for the university. That means that we are going to have to level with prospects about the pretty austere future we face. There isn't going to be money for everything we have done in the past, let alone the kinds of dreams we once had, even with a successful campaign. We are going to have to talk about some paring back to central functions, and we are going to have to argue that minority enrollments and a multicultural curriculum are right there in the center. That is not going to be easy.

TRUSTEE JONES: And we can't do without the new science building. That is clearly central, and I'm going to ask Max for that next week. The problem is, how do we raise money for the easy sells and then go on to ask for the *additional* giving needed for something like diversity that people see as nebulous at best, and quite possibly putting our quality at risk?

TRUSTEE DOE: The key here is your own word: risk. You know and I know that the donors who are most likely to come through are the venture capitalists and entrepreneurs who are not scared at all by risk, provided it makes good sense and offers big rewards. We should be completely up front with them and say we *know* putting our money on becoming a diverse university is a big gamble. But the rewards of success will be big too. Students are more and more going to want to come to a college or university that is visibly and excitingly becoming multicultural. Potential students—including those high-SAT geniuses you want—know that the world is changing. They want to be part of it, to understand it, and to feel competent in it. We should emphasize that we want to be—and can be—the best there is in fields that have a solid link with multiculturalism, such as our school of journalism, and our law and public policy program. It's all in how you bait your hook.

> Do you have ideas about how your institution can link quality and diversity in ways that are convincing to trustees, alumni, and other constituencies?

TRUSTEE SMITH: I wish you luck with your venture-capitalist friends. To our ordinary alumni, it is going to sound too much like betting the ranch on striking oil.

TRUSTEE JONES: Yes, that worries me too. I think our strongest argument may simply be that there is no better bet. We cannot pretend that a multicultural future is safe. But other futures, all things considered, are even *less* safe. Standing still is the worst bet of all. Everyone recognizes that not keeping up in science is fatal. Not keeping up with changes in our society is fatal too.

BACKGROUND ESSAY

Institutional quality is something complex that is often seen as something simple.

No one actually denies that institutional quality consists of such things as

- the intellectual competence of faculty
- the importance of their research
- the effectiveness of their teaching
- the breadth and depth of the curriculum
- the readiness of students to learn
- their achievement in learning
- the richness of life all members of the academic community bring with them
- their sharing of these experiences and perspectives in that community

Yet the conventional measures of quality are an impoverished collection: things such as SAT and GRE scores, the proportion of potential students who are *not* taught because they are denied admission, the quantity of faculty publications, the number of books in the library, the endowment per student (however the income is spent). So impoverished are the conventional measures that the most prestigious academic departments depend for self-evaluation on the rankings given them by their counterparts at *other* universities. Those institutions that have Nobel Prize winners count them, as children count baseball cards.

The quality measures in this impoverished collection interact hardly at all with the contributions a college or university makes to diversity or the contributions it *receives* from diversity. In those few instances where quality measures do interact with these contributions, there is often conflict. For example, the SAT scores of prospective minority or low-income students are often lower than what the institution feels is a "high" standard for SAT scores. The opportunities afforded by the schools and home communities of some of these students have simply made higher scores hard to come by. Not measured at all by the conventional measures are the shrewdness, courage, curiosity, and humor about a difficult world these students bring with them, nor their potential for learning that connects with their experience of life.

> ### Voice
>
> ". . . education is very much like you're sowing seeds, you know, and some of them will grow to be big trees and some won't even sprout. I think a summer bridge program can be very, very useful if you psych the students up. You bring them in and you show them the benefits of college education. You show them the work too, because you don't want someone to come in and think all they have to do is show up to get their degree, but you want them to see that education can have positives."
>
> *(Latino student)*

The conventional measures also fail to disclose how much in just these areas students of various ethnicities stand to learn from one another. Nor, of course, are there any purely academic measures of what students of *all* ethnic backgrounds will be enabled to contribute to the democratic processes of the society by reason of pursuing education together.

Not measured at all by the conventional measures are the shrewdness, courage, curiosity, and humor about a difficult world these students bring with them.

It helps to step back from the usual issues about diversity and quality and to consider two instances where extending the scope of higher education and the variety of its participants clearly has connected with excellence. The first is the land-grant colleges. They were initially intended to bring the intellectual resources of higher education to people whose motivation and social contribution were expected to be in agriculture and technology, not at all in the areas that the quality measures of, say, 1860 would have comfortably recognized. Yet they achieved institutional *and* individual excellence of immense value to the society.

Consider, second, the post-World War II GI Bill. The motivation of the legislation was a combination of democratic ideals, a sense of obligation to members of the armed services, and anxiety about what would become of veterans in the post-war world. The impulse sprang from social purpose, obligation, and concern. Yet much of the prosperity and rapid development of the United States in the 1950s and 1960s is scarcely conceivable without the individual and combined contributions that resulted from veterans' participation in higher education. The contribution of ethnic diversity in higher education will almost certainly be on the same model of interlinked individual and social benefits.

Thought Experiment

ASSESSING EDUCATIONAL PERFORMANCE

College G has traditionally admitted students with moderately high SAT scores for its largely liberal arts curriculum. It wants in the future to monitor how well it is educating an increasingly ethnically diverse student body and is considering the following alternatives:

- Require all seniors to take the GRE so that entering SATs and graduate GREs can be compared.

- Ask first-year students and seniors to write extended essays (not research papers) on topics that will give them scope to show how their views of the world have changed.

- Develop a list of skills the college wants all graduates to have, and use the best available test or other assessment vehicle for measuring the achievement of each skill.

- Ask seniors to respond to a lengthy questionnaire about what they have learned from their best teachers and from fellow students.

1. Which approach seems to you most useful and practical? What are the advantages and disadvantages of these approaches? Are there better approaches?

2. Would other approaches to assessment be appropriate for a different kind of institution?

3. How might ethnic diversity cause your institution to reconsider its methods for assessing educational effectiveness?

One aspect of the relationship between quality and ethnic diversity is even more fundamental: quality standards cannot remain static in a changing world. One parallel here is the movement in recent years to promote "computer literacy" on campus. The rationale for this movement was straightforward: with computers becoming central to a rapidly changing technological world, it would have been irresponsible not to assure students of a working familiarity with what computers can do. This was a judgment about educational quality—no education could be adequate, let alone excellent, unless it included an introduction to computers. Yet this judgment had nothing to do with the conventional criteria of quality that originated before the age of computers.

So with diversity: the ability of college graduates to function in a society of diverse ethnicities and subtle cultural differences is basic to the adequacy of their education. An excellent education will include the means to do this well, through the presence of multiple ethnicities on campus and a curriculum that develops an understanding of their differences of perspective and varied cultural contributions. Again, neither the need nor means of accomplishing the task were included in the quality standards developed for another age.

This new cultural literacy consists not only of familiarity and comfort in living in sensitive collaboration with members of other ethnic groups, although learning to do so is of immense value to the individual and to the society. It is also an intellectual competence in discerning and following ideas, comparing their validity, examining their assumptions, and interpreting the experience that lies behind them. It is an intellectual awareness of the richness of cultural life and of the interwoven historical strands that connect the great variety of cultures in the United States and the world. Such cultural literacy contributes to the in-

Thought Experiment

A CASE OF INTRUSIVE INTERVENTION

When a student at College H shows the first indication that he or she is likely to have trouble academically (either through a low score on assessment tests the first semester, or in early course grades), the student's progress is tracked relentlessly. The student's faculty advisor takes the initiative in making appointments and signs the student up for tutorials and special classes that meet frequently. One student says, "Big Brother is around every corner." Another says, "Never mind about graduating from college; what I look forward to is graduating from the intervention program." Nevertheless, the graduation rate is better than most institutions of comparable selectivity and there is no significant difference in attrition rates among the various ethnic groups on campus.

1. Is the heavy-handedness of College H justifiable?

2. Even if the heavy-handedness is justifiable, do the students in the intervention program have reasonable complaints?

3. Is there a trade-off between offering underprepared students special help and stigmatizing them, especially those who are members of minority ethnic groups?

4. Has your institution found ways to get good results without excessive intrusion?

tellectual maturation of the student both as an individual and as a responsive and responsible citizen.

Literacy, of course, is only a beginning. Beyond literacy are the opportunities for faculty to break new ground in their disciplines through following up particular strands in the multicultural web. The productivity of such investigations also stands to the credit of diversity in any reckoning of institutional quality and the vitality of intellectual community.

Thought Experiment

A MATRIX DIAGRAM

The opportunities of adapting to diversity often seem to differ by type of institution. Can you fit some of these opportunities in the matrix diagram below?

	Advantages of large institutions	Advantages of small institutions
Advantages of selective institutions	(e.g. a large array of inter-disciplinary seminars)	(e.g. residence hall–based seminars)
Advantages of non-selective institutions	(e.g. establishing strong ties with the surrounding community)	(e.g. less competitive classroom atmosphere)

REFERENCES AND RESOURCES

Access and Persistence: An Educational Program Model. Los Angeles, CA: Prism/Mount St. Mary's College.

Astin, A. W. *Achieving Educational Excellence.* San Francisco, CA: Jossey-Bass, 1985.

Finifter, D. H.; Baldwin, R. G.; and Thelin, J. R., eds. *The Uneasy Public Policy Triangle in Higher Education : Quality, Diversity, and Budgetary Efficiency.* Phoenix, AZ: American Council on Education/Oryx Press, 1991.

Infusing Multicultural Perspectives Across the Curriculum. Los Angeles, CA: Prism/Mount St. Mary's College.

Madrid, A. "Diversity and Its Discontents." *Academe.* 76(6) (Nov./Dec. 1990): 15–19.

Odell, M., and Mock, J. J., eds. *A Crucial Agenda: Making Colleges and Universities Work Better for Minority Students.* Boulder, CO: Western Interstate Commission for Higher Education, 1989. ED 310 704. Available from: WICHE Publications, P.O. Drawer P, Boulder, CO 80301-9752 (order publication number 2A180).

Reid-Wallace, C. "Access and Excellence: Are They Antithetical?" *Liberal Education* 78(2) (Mar./Apr. 1992): 22–25.

Richardson, R. C., Jr., and Skinner, E. F. *Achieving Quality and Diversity: Universities in a Multicultural Society.* Phoenix, AZ: American Council on Education/Oryx Press, 1991.

Seveland, J. *A Model for Recruitment and Retention of Minority Students for the Small College.* Washington, DC: Consortium for the Advancement of Private Higher Education, 1992.

Sources: Diversity Initiatives in Higher Education. Washington, DC: American Council on Education, 1993.

Terrel, M. C. and Wright, D. J., eds. *From Survival to Success: Promoting Minority Student Retention.* Washington, DC: National Association of Student Personnel Administrators, 1988.

COMMUNITY
AND
CAMPUS
CLIMATE

CASE

BOSK UNIVERSITY

A private university tries to deal with divisive issues connected with ethnic diversity. It does so in a context of neglected community values.

When Latino, Black, and Asian students first arrived in sizable numbers on the campus of Bosk University in the mid-1980s, you could say that the university had little sense of community, or a naive sense of community, or none at all. Twenty years earlier, Bosk had been a private comprehensive university with a regional reputation as an adequate and decent alternative to the state's public flagship university. Its national reputation was largely athletic, and its community life revolved around athletic events, sororities, fraternities, and party weekends.

In the 1960s, however, Bosk happened to have several departments that were doing world-class research, and a series of three entrepreneurial presidents pushed relentlessly for similar excellence in all areas. This effort was widely successful. External research funding amounted to 20 percent of the university's budget by 1980, and its improving academic reputation had become a recruiting advantage, somewhat more than offsetting the effects of tuition increases. This advantage permitted a considerable rise in conventional admission standards.

Bosk's improved status and visibility were gratifying to faculty and provided them with a new sense of community. They were united by the view that nothing must stand in the way of the university's newfound excellence, and they had a genuine interest in the reputation of departments other than their own. However, concentration on the university's research reputation placed concerns about the campus community, as experienced by undergraduates, beyond even the peripheral vision of most faculty. The more humble faculty would have wondered why anyone could not be content to bask in the glory of Bosk's rising star. The more arrogant would have said that community was just a matter of the right allocation of funds to bread and circuses.

Faculty in general were oblivious to a deterioration in the texture of student lives. First, an increasing proportion of courses were being taught by teaching assistants. Faculty regarded the practice as helpful in conserving their own time for research and in providing stipends for graduate students. There was little training or supervision of the T.A.'s in the actual teaching of classes. Second, for budgetary reasons, library and staff positions were not increased. In effect, the additional effort needed to serve research activities and graduate programs resulted in a reduced level of effort in undergraduate services.

The new president, appointed by the trustees in 1983, was complacent about the reputation of the university, but he was utterly serious in wanting to bring on campus many more African-American, Asian, and Latino students. He developed and implemented a very aggressive minority recruitment program. There was virtually no resistance to his program when he first proposed it, either from trustees or faculty. Some of them did not understand the program, some of them were very guarded in raising any questions about so manifestly liberal a policy, and many of them believed that the program couldn't possibly make any difference to more important things. For lack of resistance, the president did not worry much about the problems of a research-oriented faculty teaching the variety of new students or about the appearance of new cultural divisions that could hardly be bridged by a good pre-game pep rally.

As the minority recruitment program began to achieve results, those faculty who compared notes had varying impressions. Some said that students often seemed sullen in class. Some noted that minority students tended to sit together in class and to speak very little. But faculty impressions were too varied and too partial for any generalizations to be very convincing. What faculty did *not* see were some fairly common phenomena: students and T.A.'s who were mutually embarrassed by differences of accent, librarians and student aid officials too hurried to give more than the most mysterious answers to questions, and the "me first" behavior of students at bicycle racks, in dormitory television rooms, and in cafeteria lines. Nor were they aware of the small humiliations, the suppressed rages, and the cold looks. When some of these problems came out in a conversation between a Black sophomore and a disillusioned Black freshman, the sophomore said, "Nobody is saying you don't belong here, not you especially because you are Black. No one *belongs* to this university and it doesn't *belong* to anybody except the faculty. All that belongs to you is your degree—when you get it."

Some Interim Questions

Is there something fundamentally wrong with Bosk, or are there a number of little things it could set about fixing?

Would it be realistic or unrealistic to expect Bosk to have solved some of its problems of community before launching its diversity initiative?

Have students at your institution had any of the problems that students at Bosk have had?

What are some ways research-oriented faculty can be brought to think more about campus community?

In 1986 and 1987 the influx of minority students was on such a scale that White students could not be unaware that Black, Asian, and Hispanic students were taking places that some felt might have gone to their high school friends. Many White students supported the changes, but some resented that admissions requirements appeared to be lower for the new minority students, who often seemed hesitant in class. The president got wind of this resentment and asked the admissions director whether there was anything he could say to counter the resentment. The admissions director, thinking that the president wanted to deny a minority preference in admissions at all costs, offered the president some accurate but misleading figures showing that 85% of the new minority students exceeded the university's usual cut-off GPA score for high school grades, the same percentage as for Anglos. The president used this figure in several speeches.

The claim seemed implausible to an investigative journalist for the student newspaper. He did some research that found that the average SAT scores of the new students were considerably lower than those of Anglo students and that over half of the new minority students came from very troubled high schools with test scores well below the state average. The newspaper published his story under the headline "Where the New Minorities Come From: Is the Administration Lying to Us?"

These events had two consequences that made ethnic relations much more difficult. First, anything the administration thereafter said about common values and common interests across ethnic lines, no matter how accurate the supporting information given, was heavily discounted by many White students. Second, the minority students felt that the newspaper, the most nearly universal source of information on campus life, was hostile and tainted with racism. Two important voices for community values had lost much of their credibility.

The president did not like what was happening. Nor did the provost, who had once headed the public opinion research institute associated with the university. The provost suggested a series of group interviews or "focus groups" to obtain candid statements of student attitudes and assumptions.

The president and provost were appalled by the findings. Students said things like the following:

> "This isn't what I thought college would be like. It's a war game, and my color is seen as the enemy flag."

> "When I try to talk to minority students, they cut me off. They think I'm patronizing them. I know I'm not."

> "When anybody makes a mistake in class, nobody will argue with them except the professor. I mean *nobody*, because that might be taken as putting down either *us* or *them*. Each group wants to protect its own and also not to offend people who are different."

"I have got so I don't want to belong to *anything*. I hate these single ethnic groups, and, believe me, anything else is hard to find. Would you believe the World Peace Association has become an Asian club?"

"I got off to a good start with my Black roommate, but from the time we leave the dorm in the morning until late at night I never see him. Sometimes we see each other crossing the campus and we signal each other. But we never stop to talk."

"Every group is pushing for what it wants, like nobody else has a right to want anything."

"Campus politics is dead. Getting elected doesn't mean anything, just that you got the votes of a couple allied ethnic groups. Who is going to believe these guys speak for the student body?"

Some Interim Questions

Is Bosk in trouble, or is this just the normal give and take of a changing campus?

Who should have seen at an earlier point that Bosk was likely to be in trouble? What could they have done?

Is it likely that students at your institution would make statements similar to those made by the Bosk students?

What are some activities and arrangements on your campus that tend to make ethnicity more salient or less salient in student interactions?

Before any campus consensus could be reached about the seriousness of the feelings disclosed by the focus groups, or about the implications of those feelings, a series of events unfolded that further drove home how splintered the student body had become along ethnic lines and how limited were the channels of communication among the fragments. The events began with a dispute over assignments among the students who had work-study jobs in the dining halls. A few White students complained that they had been given the most menial and difficult-to-schedule assignments and that this was because the head of food service, who was an African-American woman, had intended it that way. Then African-American, Asian, and Latino students made almost identical countercharges. The various ethnic campus newspapers took up the causes of their respective groups, with cartoons showing students of each group as servants of students from other groups, or as plantation laborers with overseers who were members of other groups. All of this happened before the deeply wounded head of food service could make her case for the quite random system she actually used in making assignments. When her statement was published in the campuswide student newspaper, almost no one seemed convinced.

The president felt the campus was saved from further escalation of the dispute by the coming of examination period, when work-study schedules were made flexible in any case, as had been the practice for many years. The president was not saved, however, from a powerful sense of self-reproach. If he didn't know what to do about the fracturing of campus community, he was now humble enough to think that perhaps others would. He convened a session of his "kitchen cabinet" of administrators and faculty statesmen and asked each to bring one other person, who might or might not be a member of a minority group. The important thing was that the guest be someone who cared about the university and who had ideas.

The president opened the session by saying that it had dawned on him, with recent events, that Bosk never had been much of a community, but that it obviously needed to become one. If it succeeded, it would be a much better university, and ethnic diversity would have turned out to be a valuable gift and not the threat it now seemed to many people to be. He said, therefore, that the group should feel free to suggest fundamental reforms of structure, procedure, and expectations. The following proposals were made:

1. The dean of student affairs, a Latina with a small-college background, argued that residence halls be transformed into more effective small communities. Each could have its own social activities, mentoring programs, intramural sports, and cocurricular menu. Since the university controlled residence hall assignments, it could deliberately create intimate cross-cultural communities. Much of this could be accomplished at low cost.

2. A senior African-American faculty member who had written several books on workplace collaboration urged that courses be broken down into cross-ethnic project teams, in which each member would be seen by others as having unique usefulness to the common objective.

3. An Anglo student said, "We have had either silence or everybody yelling at one another." She suggested that a response to any future incident be planned in detail in advance. She said the university should be prepared with a plan for a campuswide "town meeting," along with plans for ethnically mixed and single ethnic forums, and a list of faculty members and administrators trained and willing to serve as discussion facilitators.

4. An Asian member of the law faculty offered the idea of developing a code of campus citizenship that would incorporate values of mutual respect, living together with consideration, frank but civil discussion of differences, and mutual support in learning. The process for development of the code should deliberately be elaborate, with many centers and occasions for its discussion.

5. A woman professor who had looked into the statistical evidence in several gender-discrimination cases and had found it highly inconclusive urged that the university adopt a "sunshine policy" that would make available the widest possible range of *good* statistics and information on university procedures, appointments, fiscal matters, and student status, limited only by a requirement not to identify individuals. Only so, she believed, could people communicate on the basis of a shared acceptance of the facts.

6. A Latino student athlete argued for a much expanded freshman orientation program, in which each student would be paired with a student of different ethnicity and both students would be taken under the wing of a paid "senior class mentor" of a third ethnicity. Frequent social and academic contacts on this basis would develop into an openness based on explicit acceptance of the values of a diverse campus community.

After the meeting, the president said to the provost, "I wish we had thought about some of these ideas five years ago."

"Yes," the provost replied, "but would we have seen the urgency?"

Some Concluding Questions for Discussion

Could the food service crisis have been used to make everyone more aware of how much they needed a better campus climate?

Do the proposals aired by the president's "kitchen cabinet" respond to the state of affairs uncovered by the focus groups? Are some of the proposals more responsive than others?

What has your campus been able to learn about itself from incidents or crises in ethnic relations?

DILEMMA

UPSILON UNIVERSITY

Faculty members debate the significance of ethnic self-segregation they see in the student dining hall.

Is there a conflict between self-segregation and educational purposes? Which educational purposes? Whose educational purposes?

Voice

". . . I felt like I was expected to join this group of Blacks, because I noticed that they were all sitting at the same table. This was the first night I went to dinner. All sitting at the same table near one corner of the dining commons, and I had met my roommate, who was Asian. I had different friends. I mean I had met all the guys on the floor, and I was thinking to myself, OK, am I going to go sit with the guys from up on the floor or go sit with the Blacks. And I felt this pulling in both directions and I was confused. I didn't know what to do and I stopped and looked and they all looked up and saw me and I was just standing there."

(Black student)

At Upsilon University, the faculty dining room is next to the student dining room. Professor A, his meal tray dominated by the meat loaf of the day, enters the faculty dining room and sits at a small table next to his friend, Professor B.

PROFESSOR A: I just walked through the student dining room and, once again, most of the Black students in the room have segregated themselves off in one corner, sitting around one large table. It bothers the hell out of me.

PROFESSOR B: I guess I take it for granted. What bothers you?

PROFESSOR A: A lot. First, the Black students aren't getting the benefit of meeting other people in the university. What's the point of having a racially integrated university if one group simply cuts itself off from everyone else? It certainly isn't what I had in mind when I was active in the civil rights movement in the sixties. Second, I'm quite sure that the Black students spend most of their time making one another feel bad about being here. It's intolerable that there is even a small amount of racism on campus, but these self-segregated groups just rub the wounds raw. Third, this self-segregation makes all of the other students feel separate and hostile. With all of the talk about diversity and respect, what we are getting on this campus is simply a hardening of the categories and a lot of suspicion among groups.

I haven't been one to talk much about political correctness. But we are obviously suffering from it, because our faculty colleagues just look the other way when we should be doing something to break these enclaves up.

(While A has been speaking, Professor C has taken the third seat at the table.)

PROFESSOR B: I guess there's something in what you say, although I've got to admit that it doesn't bother me as much as it bothers you. To be frank, those of us in engineering may be contributing to the problem, because since we discovered that Asians and White students were studying together and helping one another, we've actually encouraged first-year Hispanics and Blacks to form their own study groups. I do wonder how the Blacks feel when we sort of assign them to study in racially specific groups.

PROFESSOR A: Yes, and I wonder how they feel when they walk into the student dining room and feel that invisible pressure to sit with other Blacks at the same table. It really is a form of coercion.

> *Do other kinds of separation on campus have the same implications as students' sitting in dining halls by ethnic group? Different implications? (Consider: Staff and faculty separation, older students and younger students, resident students and commuter students, scientists and humanists.)*

PROFESSOR C: This all sounds pretty one-sided to me.

PROFESSOR A: What do you mean?

PROFESSOR C: Well, I'm a little older than either of you. I can remember as an undergraduate when Jewish students were a novelty and there was still some suspicion that they were subject to a quota. If memory serves, the Jews usually sat together at one or two tables in the dining hall. Sometimes, they still do. Let's face it, they were newcomers in a fairly large and anonymous place that had no track record of really wanting them as students, and they were under a lot of pressure to perform. So, they stuck together. No big deal. Even now, we've got a Hillel organization and a Newman Club, and the Jews and Catholics are separate from everyone else when they are active in those groups. Why don't we get excited about that?

PROFESSOR B: Point well made. Let me add something else. I know some of the kids sitting at that table. Given the fact that they are engineering majors, I'm glad they're talking to students from outside of engineering, regardless of skin color. Our students live too much in their own little disciplinary worlds.

> *Are there as many multiracial activities on your campus as there are single-race activities? More? Fewer?*

PROFESSOR C: Yes. Blackness is interdisciplinary.

PROFESSOR B: But I also want to say that, while all of those students at the table are Black, there are a lot of other differences among them, not just in majors or fields of study. Some of those students are from the Caribbean, some from big cities, some from the suburbs, some are rich and some are not, some have come from all-Black high schools and some are quite cosmopolitan. That group is not as homogeneous as we might think just from walking by the table.

Professor A: I won't deny the validity of some of what both of you have said. But, to tell the truth, both of you are dancing around the *central* question. What's happening is that "blackness" is being elevated above all of the other criteria by which people spend time with one another and develop friendships. I'm against official apartheid in South Africa, and I'm against unofficial apartheid here. In fact, some of the segregation here is official, because the campus sanctions groups like the Chinese Business Association, the Black Student Forum, and your Black study groups, B.

Would the faculty conversation have been different if all the professors present had been African Americans? What might have been said?

Professor C: Let's not get hot under the collar. Those ethnic-centered groups don't actually take up much of the lives of students, and they don't have very many members. And if they help Chinese students or others to figure this place out and make some job contacts, then I'm all for them.

Professor A: You'd sing a different tune if someone tried to start a White Students Organization.

Professor C: I'd have to think about that one for a while! But maybe if some White students wanted a separate organization, then they would be telling us that they needed some help or identification that they couldn't get otherwise. Anyway, nobody would complain about a Norwegian Student Association, and that group would certainly be lily white.

Professor B: Well, I think it is not really group identification as such that really bothers us—whether that has educational implications or not. Two other things are bothering us: First, it makes *us* feel excluded in a way that is uncomfortably new to us. Second, we are afraid that all of this racial and ethnic loyalty could somehow turn ugly and hostile toward *us*. Let's face it, we feel threatened, if only slightly. These are feelings those Black students have known all their lives. To us these feelings are new.

Professor C: Well, I'm not sure what we're getting out of this conversation except some free therapy. My only point is that self-segregation can be a form of self-help when there is no other help offered. Remember the faculty committee that looked at the first-year experience of students? The committee argued that if the university doesn't provide a reason for students to identify with a residential group, an academic department, or some activity on campus, then they'll find a "home" on campus in some other way, maybe through membership in racial and ethnic groups.

The self-segregation could well just be a passing phase, and we'll get beyond it, just as we have with religious groups on campus—at least for the most part.

PROFESSOR A: I think you're too optimistic. All of these differences are getting politicized and institutionalized. The differences aren't melting away, and if anyone is learning how to respect and value differences, as our liberal faculty colleagues would say, then it's not happening when I'm around to see it.

PROFESSOR B: You folks may have the afternoon to waste, but I've got to get to class. Two final comments. I do what I can. In my Senior Design class I try to make sure that students of different racial and ethnic backgrounds work together on projects. The students seem to like it—I've never had a complaint. And you can be damn sure they're spending some time out of class working together to finish those projects! And, here's the other thing. I wonder what those students in the other room are saying about us.

BACKGROUND ESSAY

"The biggest obstacle to building community at this college is the belief that we already have one," says a college president.

This college president could be speaking for many institutions. Part of the problem is that colleges tend to *look* like communities and *feel* like communities to those students and faculty who find that the priorities of the institution affirm their own. But a divisive issue can challenge such complacency, testing the capacity for trust and communication that are basic to community. Colleges and universities would do well to find out how much sense of community really exists and to consider how that sense of community can be strengthened before such challenges come.

Voice

"I had never noticed the racial differences so much until I got (here). . . . There are big differences, and these people will point them out to you, telling you you got in only because of affirmative action. They make you feel small."

Ethnic diversity can give rise to such challenges. One reason is that people of traditional college-going age are just not that easy to deal with on issues of community norms. The developmental tasks of late adolescents create tensions and ambivalence about belonging to *any* community. The result can be various divisions of the campus between "us" and "them," with respect and support for "us" and denial of these basic needs to "them." Because the "us" and the "them" may be ethnic categories, colleges and universities engaging diversity often find that they must confront major tasks of community building and not just tasks of minor adjustment and accommodation.

A fundamental task of all community building, highlighted by efforts on behalf of diversity, is to come to terms with how people feel about one another, and how their feelings enhance or obstruct their participation in the community and the pursuit of its goals. These include feelings

- about being considered worthy of attention and concern
- about the responsiveness of others
- about the degree of personal respect accorded by others
- about "superior" or "inferior" roles in collaborations
- about indicia of privilege and status
- about language and other vehicles of communication
- about the validity of mutual demands and expectations

Feelings about such things are as basic to any community architecture as is the strength of materials to a building. This fact runs up against a residual puritanism in many colleges and universities. It is commonplace for actions on behalf of diversity to be scorned as "feel good" activities.

No effort to expand academic communities to include members of diverse ethnic groups is likely to get very far on premises that deny the relevance of emotion and feelings.

There is a persistent sense that some suffering is good for you, that feelings are something to be overcome, not accommodated, and that everyone should try hard and be valued only by their intellectual achievements. These attitudes are common among some academics when the topic is students in general or minorities in general, even though the same academics would be horrified at the idea of conducting one-to-one relationships of any kind on this basis.

No effort to expand academic communities to include members of diverse ethnic groups is likely to get very far on premises that deny the relevance of emotion and feelings. Many people find it easier to think about the role of feelings in such a transition if they consider the experiences of their ancestors who were immigrants. Feelings of rejection, humiliation, or defiance were commonplace among immigrants, as were feelings of insecurity and powerlessness. Immigrants from many different countries had feelings of guilt about abandoning the ways and the language of "the old country." Much of what European immigrants did and suffered in the nineteenth and early twentieth centuries only makes sense as an effort—often triumphant—to deal with this range of feelings. We should obviously expect Hispanics and Asians, some of whom are in fact of recent immigrant origin, to have such feelings and to focus major energies on coping with them. African Americans, although they have mostly been in the United States geographically for a very long time, have, up to the present day, been treated as marginal—and have experienced many, if not all, of the same feelings.

It is perhaps useful to think about members of any of these ethnic groups arriving on campus as having a state of mind similar in many respects to that of new immigrants arriving at Ellis Island or at a Texas border town or finding a first American home in an Asian urban enclave. There are similar possibilities of feeling accepted only on a kind of probation whose requirements are mysterious

Thought Experiment

AN ANNUAL PICNIC

College I is blessed with spectacular scenery in the neighborhood of the campus. An annual event for the student body is a picnic on one of the lakes. However, few Black students attend the event. They say it is "not their kind of party," and the Black Student Association proposes an alternative event.

1. Should the college give the same degree of quasi-official sanction to both the lakeside and alternative events?

2. Would it matter whether the alternative event is exclusively for Black students or whether Black students would be the hosts for an event with wider participation?

3. How do you know what students feel about cross-ethnic interactions in social settings on your campus?

4. Would an alternative graduation ceremony be a similar or a different case? Why?

and easily misunderstood, of having no road map for arrangements and relationships that others take for granted, of feeling manipulated by decisions being made on their behalf without having a voice in them that is listened to or understood. These feelings can take over in the most commonplace situations: a residence hall assignment, a first meeting with a faculty advisor, an assignment to do some library research, or having to find the money called for by the student aid office as a "self-help" contribution to college expenses.

It does not help at all that a White student whose parents, friends, and neighbors went to college can readily imagine the reasons for things that confuse or humiliate a first-generation student. Students whose parents went to college commonly know the kinds of thing to expect, know when and how to protest arrangements that are probably negotiable, and know the kinds of demands they can make in their own interest that will probably be respected. Living alongside such students may only make the new arrival feel more inadequate and disadvantaged. Most freshmen feel miserable a good deal of the time, but first-generation students can easily feel that it is their special fate and perceive it as prejudice or racism.

That is, until the new arrival learns these things from other students who "know the ropes." At those institutions that are already blessed with a strong sense of community before they take on the tasks of diversity, it may not be that hard for juniors and seniors to pass on such knowledge to freshmen, minority students included. Adequate mechanisms for transmitting that kind of information may already be in place. But in large institutions that have little sense of campuswide community, a formal or informal ethnic network can provide some of the comforts of home, just as the immigrant societies of the nineteenth century gave both practical and emotional support. Such networks will tend to increase pride in ethnic identity, and the more the other practices of the campus can be seen as disparaging that identity, the more the network is likely to insist on its value.

Thought Experiment

RIGHTS VS. OPPORTUNITIES

Which of the following are rights of ethnic minority students by virtue of their presence on campus and which are opportunities a college may—or may not—choose to provide in the light of its judgment of how much each contributes to goals of community and academic achievement?

- **clear official statements of institutional policy on racial and gender harassment**

- **meeting facilities for ethnic-exclusive student associations**

- **opportunities to raise money for an ethnic newspaper**

- **proportional time on the campus radio station for broadcasts of ethnically oriented news and entertainment**

- **faculty advisor assignments based on ethnic group identification**

- **availability of an ethnic studies major**

- **dining hall food in each student's ethnic tradition**

> *Most freshmen feel miserable a good deal of the time, but first-generation students can easily feel that it is their special fate and perceive it as prejudice or racism.*

A sense of community, or the lack of it, is expressed and transmitted in many small events, in feelings about the attitudes exemplified in the minutiae of campus life and in perceptions about the fairness and supportiveness of others' behavior. Just as the weather depends on the cumulative effect of innumerable small events in the atmosphere, so does campus climate. Such events might include positively:

- having one's contribution to a study group fairly appreciated

- the manner of a librarian that shows respect for the seriousness of a student's inquiry

- instances of good humor in sharing the trials and benefits of the same residence hall

- staff behavior that shows it is legitimate to have problems in coping with campus arrangements

- hearing a professor having an animated and amusing conversation with another student of the hearer's ethnicity

- noticing a plaque honoring a personal cultural hero

Such events might also include negatively:

- a glance at an offensively worded headline in the campus newspaper

- remarks disparaging one's culture overheard while standing in line with other students

Thought Experiment

A CASE OF VANDALISM

A third act of vandalism has occurred at the Asian student center of College J. In the first, posters and announcements from the center's bulletin board were taken down and switched with similar materials taken from the Black student center. In the second incident, all vending machines at the Asian student center were made inoperable.

The culprits were not identifiable in either of these two cases. The president of the college decided to ignore both incidents, on the advice of the widely trusted dean of students, who thought they were innocuous pranks, quite possibly perpetrated by Asian students themselves.

The third incident had strong overtones of racial animosity. All the furniture from the Asian student center's main meeting room was moved out of the center and arranged in front of a widely ridiculed ornamental structure referred to on campus as "the Pagoda."

1. If the culprits are found, should the college take action against them on the basis of regulations designed to deal only with property damage, in the absence of regulations against ethnic ridicule?

2. Should the dean of students have taken the earlier incidents more seriously because they occurred at the Asian student center, even without clear racist intent?

3. Who on your campus should take responsibility for noticing warning signs of racial antagonism?

- a professor's phrasing of a question that suggests low expectations of the respondent

- social arrangements based upon an unspoken assumption that friendships and affection will not cross racial and ethnic lines

Such perception-laden events are cumulatively of immense importance to community, but they are sometimes on so small a scale as to be individually almost invisible. This is one of the reasons faculty and senior administrators are often so surprised at the way events surrounding diversity unfold. They sometimes simply don't see what minority students see: a mosaic of small incidents that add up to a picture of an alienating, nonsupportive environment.

Casual observation of such small events can sometimes be astute and illuminating, but it is hard to know whether such observations are looking at a meaningful sample of relevant events. To know what responsible faculty members and administrators need to know, entirely casual observation is bound to be inadequate. It is not the special nature of engaging diversity that causes this problem. *Any* effort to investigate seriously the state of community values would run up against the same problem of knowing enough of what actually goes on.

Campus climate is the formal and informal environment, both institutionally and community-based, in which individuals learn, teach, work, and live. What is called for might be termed "an adequately structured

> ### *To know what responsible faculty members and administrators need to know, entirely casual observation is bound to be inadequate.*

assessment" of this campus climate. Where time, resources, and purposes indicate, such an assessment can be provided by the statistically sophisticated collection of data on the kinds of experiences and expectations students and employees have and their feelings about them. Faculty who have expertise in such data collection and analysis can be invaluable here. But the important thing is to be sure that major groups and major areas of community experience are not left out. In the end it is the *whole* community, involving all its parts, that needs to be understood and strengthened.

A study of community climate may be statistically biased by oversampling or undersam–

Thought Experiment

COMMUNITY INDICATORS

Whether or not a college decides to make deliberate efforts to assess campus climate concerning diversity matters, are there statistics or other information routinely collected for other purposes that may shed light on campus climate? (Consider data collected routinely in the registrar's office, the student aid office, libraries, student services, dining halls, and bookstores.)

pling, by self-selection, and by imitative responses and still provide very useful information, but such a study cannot be adequately structured if major areas of campus life are neglected. For students, it is essential to explore feelings about classroom interchange, purely social occasions, residence arrangements, use of dining and other facilities, participation in group activities (including study groups), and both intra-ethnic and cross-ethnic contacts. For staff, some of these topics will be appropriate along with questions about hiring practices, how employees are evaluated, and the opportunities provided for professional development and advancement. Contacts between staff and faculty, and between staff and students are often especially revealing about the extent to which community values are not just for show.

There are many techniques for conducting such a study, ranging from questionnaires to group interviews and focus groups to task forces. A selection among these techniques should be made on the basis of the information and kind of communication sought. Questionnaires have important uses in studies of campus climate because they can give statistically valid results. As with all surveys, it is important to ask the right questions—ones that do not bias results and that are likely to differentiate perceptions rather than produce large percentages of agreement or disagreement with vague formulations. An important value of questionnaires is the possibility of repeating a survey after an interval,

---

Thought Experiment

A CASE OF STUDENT POLITICS

At the University of K, the executive committees of the Black Student Association and the Chicano Student Association agree to create a joint political party for student government elections. They further agree to divide the party's nominations for office strictly according to the university's official head count of members of the two ethnic groups.

1. Is this action an indication that Black and Chicano students are entering the mainstream of campus life or that they are not?

2. Can competition among ethnic groups contribute to a sense of community if it is a community-wide competition, as in intramural athletics or debate?

3. Could this be an example of such constructive competition?

It is important to remember that surveys correspond roughly to taking a person's temperature periodically and do not by themselves indicate appropriate diagnosis and treatment.

---

and thereby finding out whether the campus climate has grown more or less supportive of diversity. For this reason most questions should be framed in a way that will be as meaningful to a later group of students and employees as to the present one. For example, questions should avoid reference to an event that few will have witnessed or discussed five years from now. It is important to remember that surveys correspond roughly to taking a person's temperature periodically and do not by themselves indicate appropriate diagnosis and treatment.

Many campuses will use other techniques for assessing campus climate, either to prepare for a survey or instead of a survey. Techniques such as individual interviews, group interviews, or focus groups provide an opportunity to determine immediately which are the salient topics to explore. These techniques also allow institutions to investigate how people have arrived at their conclusions, both their evidence and their reasoning from the evidence. The *kind* of evidence adduced may also be important to the assessment of campus climate. For example, if many more students cite contacts with the campus bureaucracy as evidence for their perceptions about diversity than cite the classroom behavior of professors, then this may authorize the conclusion that bureaucratic contacts, at least on this campus, are a more sensitive area than administrators may have known, and more deserving of priority attention.

Another great advantage of group interviews and focus groups is that they enhance communication. Members of the campus community who participate in these interviews become much more aware and sensitive about the feelings and perceptions of other ethnic groups. For this reason, it is valuable to use both mixed- and single-ethnic groups in a group discussion format. It is valuable not only to find out about the perceptions of others but to be in their presence when they express their perceptions. Such direct exposure brings out the hearer's capacity for empathy in a way that percentages in a poll cannot. At the same time, such face-to-face contacts provide an opportunity for people expressing perceptions to search for ways of rephrasing their own words to achieve better empathic communication. Feelings and attitudes initially expressed in borrowed or hackneyed formulas can be replaced by more deeply felt and more communicative words.

Face-to-face contacts provide an opportunity for people expressing perceptions to search for ways of rephrasing their own words to achieve better empathic communication.

When used to enhance communication in these ways, group interviews and focus groups can be seen as on a continuum between questionnaire surveys and the work of a campuswide task force on campus climate that seeks both to bring out awareness of community values and to modify them in the interest of a closer, more mutually supportive community. Such a task force can, indeed, serve very useful purposes of fact finding. But it can also be a process for hearing many voices in formulating topics of investigation, so that the questions themselves enshrine a new sensitivity to the experience of various groups. It is sometimes desirable to build several stages into a task-force process, with many forums and stages of review, so that a transformation of campus climate will be set in train even while it is being investigated, and so that appreciation of the value of diversity will be enhanced. Although such a process is not formal social science, it can result in much insight and information.

There are instances where such a process has uncovered important strengths as well as weaknesses of campus community. These strengths have included reservoirs of goodwill of which many people were unaware. They have included campus activities, previously inconspicuous, that promote cross-cultural collaboration—for example, ethnically mixed student project teams for dealing with regular course assignments.

The word *community* is indispensable in discussing the issues raised in the foregoing, because there seems to be no other word that generically calls to mind the mutuality of support, respect, and accommodation that enables people to live and work together on nonauthoritarian terms. When we speak of an academic community, however, it is easy to imagine that the model for community is the small, cohesive residential college. It is, indeed, in some ways an excellent model, because the life of such institutions underscores that there is something in an academic community that all participants—faculty and staff as fully as students—can feel they belong to. The small-college model also underlines how community values can be used to reinforce academic values.

Most students probably attend institutions that have experienced very rapid change very recently — in their curricula, in their financing, and in their relationship with surrounding nonacademic communities, as well as in their ethnic composition.

Most students today, however, attend much larger institutions that are residential only in part, if at all. Many students are older, with adult commitments that reduce the time, energy, and need to form the kinds of interpersonal bonds small colleges have traditionally encouraged. A good many students attend specialized institutions that provide highly specific contexts for community values. Furthermore, most students probably attend institutions that have experienced very rapid change very recently—in their curricula, in their financing, and in their relationship with surrounding nonacademic communities, as well as in their ethnic composition. In such circumstances, campus values can receive little reinforcement from the patina of time and custom that is associated with the small college.

Even so, a sense of mutuality and belonging is still essential. When a first-generation ethnic minority student takes her place in her first class at an enormous urban institution (for which she may have registered by voice mail), she needs to feel that the instructor and her fellow students accept her presence as a par-

Thought Experiment

A CAFETERIA INCIDENT

A male student is irritated by the slowness of the female student ahead of him in line as she makes up her mind about a choice of salads. He says, "Hurry up, you _____ _____," where one of the two epithets is racial and one is sexual.

1. Would it make the incident less offensive to a sense of community if both students were of the same gender?

2. Would it make the incident less offensive to a sense of community if both students were of the same ethnic group?

3. If a rumor went around the campus that the two students were of different races and genders, and the administration found out that they were of the same race and gender, how should it make the facts known? Could the different permutations of the case be used to get students to think about what is involved in such incidents? How?

ticipant who will both give and receive in the learning process that is underway and who will be respected and supported in both. These needs are basic, whatever the type of institution, and they have nothing to do with the amount of ivy growing up the walls.

Each institution needs to reflect on the situations of its typical students in deciding on its goals as an ethnically diverse community, without assuming that these goals will be the same for all institutions, except in such fundamental respects. Nor should all institutions assume that they will be achievable by the same means. Students have various levels of contact with a campus community, from the once-a-week class to full-time residential enrollment, and these levels will necessarily affect their level of involvement with other students, whether of the same or other ethnicities. There can also be several levels of multicultural contact, each ascending level having value: tolerance of difference, acceptance of another person's attachment to his or her culture, intellectual appreciation of that culture, and a sense of being personally enriched by contacts with that culture.

The activities that are accepted as typically for single-ethnic or multiethnic participation can also vary. Just as leisure relationships in the wider society are commonly single-ethnic but workplace relations multiethnic, so campus recreational groups can often be single-ethnic at the same time that the institution insists that classroom relationships be on the basis of the fullest sharing in activities.

The situations of those students of multiethnic ancestry are worth special attention as these levels of involvement and contact are considered. Such ancestry can confront a student, faculty member, or staff employee with awkward choices and can inflict a painful sense of isolation if ethnic lines are sharply drawn. Accepting and valuing these members of the community can, on the other hand, provide their peers with useful and encouraging examples of interethnic and intercultural bridges.

These many dimensions of community on a diverse campus can be disrupted by tensions that differ in degree of destructiveness. A lack of responsiveness on the part of faculty and other students gives rise to one level of tension. Habitual and negligent incivility is obviously worse, recklessly or intentionally wounding behavior worse still. When unacceptable behavior at any level gives rise to a publicized incident, it is worth considering whether discussion of the incident can be used to make all members of the campus community more aware of the feelings and values at stake. If misunderstandings or distortion by rumor have played a part, all concerned can be enabled to learn better ways to deal with such phenomena. Making use of an incident for such purposes—even an incident the institution profoundly wishes never had happened—is likely to have much better results than denial, disavowal, or minor palliatives. Failure to do so can leave those who might be injured uncertain about the kind of treatment they have a right to expect. Lack of clarity about such matters can also give rise to persistent and damaging misunderstandings. Students of differing ethnic backgrounds, for example, may say emphatically that they are against racism, but the particular behaviors that they would label as racist can be quite different.

No matter what kind of institution, it is important to make institutional norms about such matters clear to *all* faculty, staff, and students. Too often incidents, grievances, or demands for exclusive rights of association are treated as disputes between only two parties—members of a single-ethnic group and the campus administration. In fact, interests of all groups are usually at stake, and all groups can be called upon to make their special contributions to the livability and academic excellence of the community as a whole.

REFERENCES AND RESOURCES

General

Resource Guide for Assessing Campus Climate. Sacramento, CA: California Postsecondary Education Commission, 1992. Commission Report 92-24.

Spitzberg, I. J., and Thordike, V. V. *Creating Community on College Campuses.* Albany, NY: State University of New York Press, 1992.

Thank You for Asking! Using Focus Groups to Improve Minority Participation. Washington, DC: National Institute of Independent Colleges and Universities, 1991. ED 342 862.

Tierney, W. G., ed. *Assessing Academic Climates and Cultures.* New Directions for Institutional Research, no. 68. San Francisco, CA: Jossey-Bass, 1990.

Toward an Understanding of Campus Climate: A Report to the Legislature in Response to Assembly Bill 4071. Sacramento, CA: California Postsecondary Education Commission, 1990. Commission Report 90-19.

Understanding Campus Climate: An Approach to Supporting Student Diversity. Washington, DC: National Institute of Independent Colleges and Universities, 1991.ED 342 864.

Campus Studies

Abraham, A. A. *Racial Issues on Campus: How Students View Them.* Atlanta, GA: Southern Regional Education Board, 1990. ED 328 180.

Astin, A. W., Trevino, J. G., and Wingard, T. L. *UCLA Campus Climate for Diversity.* Los Angeles, CA: Higher Education Research Institute, UCLA, 1991.

California Legislature, Senate. Special Committee on University of California Admissions, Art Torres, chairman. *Hearing on Racial/Ethnic Tensions and Hate Violence on University of California Campuses.* Sacramento, CA: [The Committee], [1989].

The Diversity Project. Berkeley, CA: Institute for the Study of Social Change, University of California, Berkeley, 1991.

James, O. C. R., ed. *Final Report of the University Commission on Human Relations: Focus on Racism and Other Forms of Discrimination.* San Francisco, CA: San Francisco State University, 1990. 7 vols. ED 323 885-91.

Stanford University, Committee on Minority Issues. *Building a Multiracial, Multicultural University Community: Final Report of the University Committee on Minority Issues.* Palo Alto, CA: Stanford University, 1989.

Reports of such studies based on the experience of smaller institutions include those of the Master's College and Seminary, Newhall, CA; Mount St. Mary's College, Los Angeles, CA; and Westmont College, Santa Barbara, CA.

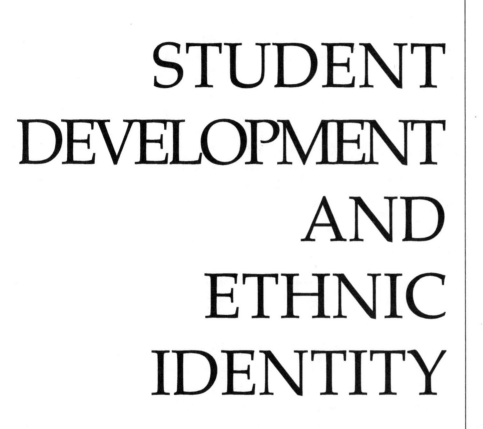

STUDENT DEVELOPMENT AND ETHNIC IDENTITY

CASE

LEE JONES

An African-American sophomore is alienated and discouraged by the events of his day. He is thinking about dropping out.

Lee Jones was late to his statistics class again that day. He had never been late for the first period in high school (his mother had seen to that), nor had he often been late to classes in his freshman year. But now, in his sophomore year, it was different. He felt slowed down. Maybe he should ask for a checkup at the student health service.

At first he had been terrified of being late for class. That White guy who was always laughing, as though he had the secret of everything, said that

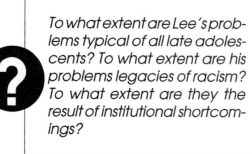

To what extent are Lee's problems typical of all late adolescents? To what extent are his problems legacies of racism? To what extent are they the result of institutional shortcomings?

if you were late, it was a sure thing the instructor would call on you. Well, that hadn't been Lee's experience. No one called on him when he was late, so he wasn't terrified anymore, he just felt angry. It was as though it didn't matter to the instructor whether he was there or not, on time or not. He mattered less than whether he was in the audience at a movie. The instructor somehow couldn't see a Black student being interested in statistics.

Lee had thought statistics would be an important course. In the textbook for his first-year social science core course, there had been a table on almost every page, showing how groups were alike and yet different from one another. Being able to see and explain such things would be really worth something. But this course! When the instructor talked about people, he made it clear that it was only to give himself an excuse to talk about some new formula. His favorite examples were about green and blue men on Mars, and how you

could find out if short green ones had better ESP than tall blue ones. He would use such examples looking out at a class where all the Blacks sat at the back of the room. He was thinking about color, all right, but color was something you did statistics *about* rather than people you did statistics *with*.

Would someone know if students on your campus were as discouraged and alienated as Lee? How would someone know?

The first week of classes, another Black student in the statistics class had asked, "What is the probability of a Black student getting an 'A' in this course?" Lee guessed he was making a joke, maybe not. But the instructor had been totally embarrassed, all the White students, too. Not a word was said, but you could sure read the silence: the answer was "Zero."

Well, Lee was proving that this was the right answer. When class was over, he had to turn to the woman next to him even to find out what the next assignment was. Somehow, he had ended up spending most of the hour thinking about home. He wished his sister would go ahead and get married. She was driving their mother crazy. But this guy she was going with was nowhere near good enough for her.

Lee came out into the courtyard in front of the social sciences building feeling a little shaky and blinded by the glare. Then he remembered he had to see his faculty advisor. This guy knew where to sign his course card, and that's about all. Lee was thinking about dropping out, but he wasn't going to bring that up. It would be easy to avoid talking about anything important. This guy was a professor of Italian literature and always wanted to talk about his last trip to Florence or Perugia.

The advisor's office was piled to the ceiling with books. Just seeing all the books this guy had read was pretty impressive at first. Then Lee had a fantasy that there could be an earthquake and all of the books could come down on top of them like an avalanche. Not that it would make any difference to this guy. He was buried alive already. But not Lee, not yet anyway.

After Lee got his card signed he went along to the cafeteria. Phil, the president of the Black Student Association, was at his usual table, wearing a red beret as always. Lee had looked up to Phil from the first time he had attended one of the BSA meetings. Phil had a way of making every miserable little thing about this place some kind of joke. You laughed, and then you felt you were breathing fresh air at last. At Phil's table it was a little like being in Lee's old high school. In high school, if people saw you as different or special, it wasn't because you were a different color, because almost everyone had been the *same* color.

The trouble was, Phil was now spending all his time on an article for the campus newspaper. There were endless revisions, as though he never really wanted to finish it. Each draft started with the idea that all Black students had the same problems with the university, which Lee knew wasn't true. The article went on to say that the university was racist and explained all the reasons why this was inevitable. Then each draft went on with a long timetable of demands, listing just what the administration must do and when. Well, if it was all a joke, and everything was inevitable, what was the point of a timetable? Better just to get out of here, and that was what Lee was going to do.

> *How can discouraged students themselves take initiatives to change their situations on your campus? For example, how might a student like Lee have engaged his faculty advisor?*

> *Who on your campus has the job of helping resolve individual students' problems of the kinds Lee is encountering? Consider teaching faculty, administrators, advisors, and service staff. Do they have a clear mandate to take action in such cases? Do they have the training and support they may need?*

DILEMMA

IOTA UNIVERSITY

At issue is whether the needs of ethnic minority students are specific to their groups, or similar for all late adolescents. The context is a discussion of staff assignments in a counseling center.

The scene is the regular Monday morning meeting of the counseling staff of the student services center of Iota University. The group picks up on a discussion it has pursued for some time without resolution: whether Black, Hispanic, and Asian students should ordinarily be seen by counselors from the same ethnic group.

MR. O: There are three reasons for figuring out some way to match students and their counselors. To me, they seem overwhelming. First, only a member of the same ethnic group can possibly know what the student is going through—the way I know what it is like to be a scared Latino kid because I *was* one. The second is the need for trust. It takes a counselor of the same group to forge an alliance with the student in working through his problems. Otherwise, how can the student believe the counselor is on his side? The third reason is that a counselor of the same ethnic group can know what resources are available for a student belonging to a particular ethnic group, both on and off campus.

Do the problems noted in the dilemma also occur in student-to-student relationships? In student-to-faculty relationships?

DR. N: Maybe you can convince me on your first two points, but you are plainly wrong on the third. It is our *job* to know what resources are available. If you know and the rest of us don't, then tell us.

MS. R: Does it have to be so complicated, a federal case? No one is suggesting that we do anything different in principle from what we do in dealing with women. The health service—wisely, I think—has only women gynecologists. And the rape crisis center hardly has men as counselors!

DR. N: But there are biological and deep psychological reasons for these arrangements. I don't see differences that great among ethnic groups.

DR. M: Well, I do. Take the case of Black students. Who but another Black can understand what it is like to grow up Black in the United States today? If you are Black, chances are your family represented security with discipline, the life of the streets represented freedom with palpable danger, and television represented all the things you weren't allowed ever to have. By junior high you were being told by every communication from the White world that it was your fault that life was like this. There was something about being different and Black that put you in the low-achievement track in school and that made other parts of town hostile to you.

MR. O: Yes, and if you are a Latino, by the time you were in high school you were hungry for things to be proud of, people who considered you normal, and places that were less threatening. You were in a permanent state of siege. Wisdom, wherever it came from, was what enabled you to survive in siege conditions. It was foolish to add to your already great risks, or to open old wounds. It somehow seemed subversive of your survival strategies for anyone to suggest by word or example that the world was actually more open than you had been trained to think, that education was such an opening. Now, who can understand all of this who has not experienced it? Plainly, most Whites do not.

DR. N: But you two understand each other, and we *all have to* understand. Again, it is our *job*. If we don't understand, you are going to have to help us to.

MR. O: It isn't that easy. For example, you know how many people on this campus dismiss truly wounding encounters with racism as trivial. They discount the siege mentality as just paranoia. Don't you sometimes react that way? Doesn't that reaction sometimes affect what you do?

DR. N: Didn't we all learn in graduate school that paranoia is never "just paranoia." I feel a commitment to take every student seriously.

MR. O: But can a Latino student who comes in for counseling have confidence that you do? He needs to feel that the full force of the Latino experience is understood without its being put into words. For example, a Latino student, male or female, needs a counselor who will not push him or her toward taking risks without also being able to find the means to limit those risks and to assure a refuge of emotional support in case things go badly. A Latino counselor can offer this kind of understanding, alliance, and access to the supports required. A White counselor, on the other hand, knows nothing of all this.

DR. M: And chances are, he doesn't realize that he doesn't know. He offers advice like a tennis coach. He doesn't realize that he is suggesting anything more dangerous than a way to improve the student's backhand. But the Black student can easily feel he is being urged to take up bungee jumping.

> *Do the issues raised by the counseling staff mainly concern problems of communication with students or the substance of students' problems?*

DR. N: But that would be a mistake *with any student*. The experiences you have recounted can be described, as you have done, in terms specific to Latino or Black students. But I could describe each and every one of them in terms descriptive of the typical experience of *all* late adolescents. We all, in those years, have to sort out the things that make us secure and the things that are dangerous.

All adolescents feel, with some reason, that the adult world is inherently dangerous, and they are all grabbing for parachutes and clinging to the oddest remnants of childhood so they can delay making the jump. A siege mentality is just one manifestation of the general phenomenon. It reflects the common fears and also the common protective strategies of group solidarity and the cherishing of specialness.

How do you assess the relative importance of general student development issues versus issues specific to students of each ethnic group?

We could go on and on matching up typical minority experiences and typical experiences of adolescents per se. I am sure you could describe to us vividly typical cases of depression among Asian students and terror of authority among many groups of recent immigrants. But each and every one of these phenomena would be but a special case of general patterns common among all students. We have all been professionally trained, thank God, to deal reasonably well with these common situations, to diagnose what is going on and to nudge students back on track.

Mr. P: I tend to agree. I think in terms of the academic and career counseling that I do. All college students have the same problem of finding some match between the things they fantasize about doing with their lives and the things they are especially good at, which they usually don't know yet. You could cite cases of African-American students tormenting themselves about whether to take a career path that would serve the Black community or one that could lead to a lucrative career beyond the community. True, this is an especially agonizing choice for many African-American students, but it is no different in kind from the torments of the Chinese American trying to decide whether to join the family business or not, or the Latina torn by the feeling that she should forgo graduate school to be a support to her family. Loyalty, and guilt about disloyalty, are part of what adolescence is all about.

Ms. R: I think the argument for same-group counselors is strongest on the point of gaining the trust of minority students. As our society is now, there often really are barriers to trust between ethnic groups. The barriers can be broken down, but by a process that is too time-consuming when needs are immediate.

Mr. P: But be careful, even here. Just matching up counselors and students by broad ethnic categories will often not be enough. The Blacks on our staff are mostly from middle-class West Coast families. Would they really know enough intuitively to gain the trust of a Haitian student or one from a small town in Louisiana? Would a third-generation Chinese American necessarily have that much instant rapport with a recently arrived Cambodian? With Hispanics, of course, the possibilities of mismatch are endless: Cubans, Puerto Ricans, Mexicans, and Guatemalans, rich, poor, rural, urban—all represent distinctive experiences of life.

Ms. R: I still think we are making the whole thing too complicated. The problem is a lot easier and also a lot harder than any of you are suggesting.

The practical question of same-group counseling is the easy part. Why not have an arrangement where the first appointment is taken by a counselor of the same ethnic group—and gender—if one is available? If not, the receptionist can ask whether the student will see whatever counselor is available or wants to wait in order to meet with a counselor of the same group. The receptionists have the tact to do this comfortably, and I hope we have the tact to know when it would, or would not, be advisable to shift cases after the first interview to even up the load.

We don't have to have one strict rule or another about appointments, except for *one* rule, and that is not to get uptight about any of our arrangements. A counselor that is uptight about issues of ethnicity will not create a comfortable environment and is quite likely to miss things he or she should hear.

And that brings me to my second point, about what is so difficult with the issue, not just as it applies to the counseling staff, but as it applies to the whole university. We are too tense, and so is the whole university, about issues of ethnicity. We need to provide a kind of counseling to faculty, staff, and students in general so that they will be less tense and more prepared to "play it by ear" in the best sense.

What practices and arrangements on your campus make growing up easier or harder for ethnic minority students? For White students?

Dr. N: Yes, that is basic. We need to get across that everybody has some growing to do, that the point of having undergraduates at a university is to allow and promote growth, and that we can take most of the hazards of growth in stride.

BACKGROUND ESSAY

Risks faced by *all* late adolescents can become incorporated into ethnic stereotypes.

Consider four stories:

One freshman remains profoundly homesick all year.

A second receives a D and threatens suicide.

A third takes an extra heavy course load to graduate early, even though her grades will probably suffer.

A fourth joins a large number of organizations and runs for office in student government as soon as she can.

The miseries of the first and second of these students are familiar to student affairs personnel and to some faculty. The possibly shortsighted behavior of the third and fourth are familiar too. Each of the four is an example of the hazards of growing up, reactions to a process that most adults are thankful they have outgrown. Ethnicity does not enter the picture so far. But suppose we are told that the first freshman is a Black woman: A wellworn (surely unfounded) stereotype instantly clicks into place. This is just the kind of problem a young Black woman might be expected to have. Again, suppose we are told that the second student is Asian. Yes, of course, Asian students are (supposedly) devastated by poor grades. If the third student is said to be a Latina, this also fits with a preconception. Doesn't she want to graduate quickly so that she will be a burden on her family for as little time as possible? And if the fourth student is said to be White, this "fits" too: she is the well-known joiner.

> ### Voice
>
> *"I'd never heard anyone use the word Anglo for me before . . . where I came from, no one was Anglo; everyone was just Irish Catholic. But after being (here) a while, I realized that an Anglo can be an Anglo only if there's someone who's not."*
>
> *(White woman student)*

What this exercise illustrates is how easily risks faced by *all* late adolescents can become incorporated into ethnic stereotypes. Although homesickness, depression, anxiety about money, and unfocused ambition can afflict any student, *and we know this,* we find it amazingly comfortable to assume an affinity between particular ethnic groups and particular issues of student development.

Not only do faculty and staff do this, students do this to members of other groups, to members of their own group, even to themselves. For example, some Asian students worry about the part of their grade point average to the right of the decimal point because they feel, as Asians, that they are supposed to. These tendencies to stereotype are moderated, of course, by the awareness of members of an ethnic group of the tremendous variety *within* the group, a variety nonmembers of the group may more easily ignore. These tendencies are moderated also by the development of important friendships between members of different groups, but only moderated, because often a friend in another ethnic group is regarded as an "exception" to the stereotype, not a refutation.

The net result of stereotyping is that general phases of growing up are often articulated and underscored, as though they belonged especially or exclusively to members of a particular ethnic group. If other members of the campus community take such phenomena at face value, stereotypes can become entrenched, even though the phenomena may make the most sense when viewed in terms of what younger students of all ethnic backgrounds most clearly have in common, namely, their youth. The point here is not that we must choose between seeing all students as the same and seeing separate ethnic patterns of growing up, but that we can see different responses and motivations as permutations and variations on general themes.

Broad identifications mask an even greater variety in the life experiences that have given them content: experiences of opportunity or frustration, valued or demeaned status, isolation or solidarity with others.

When the tendency to think in terms of stereotypes is set aside, what is seen is immense variety. Part of this variety is along dimensions faculty have seen for a very long time—euphoria and discouragement, focused energy and aimlessness, hard work and idleness. But there is also variety in the identifications of each individual student. One and the same student may see herself as a woman, a Latina, a student leader, a rising professional, and a Republican. Context may tend to push one identification rather than another to the fore at a particular moment, but others are not very far from expression. These broad identifications mask an even greater variety in the life experiences that have given them content: experiences of opportunity or frustration, valued or demeaned status, isolation or solidarity with others. Identifications may be seen as a privilege or as a burden, and there is a dimension of tension or reinforcement among identifications: being a student and a member of higher education's culture can feel supportive or antagonistic to other identities rooted in one's family and home neighborhood.

Thought Experiment

A CASE OF TRADING EPITHETS

An older White male professor of history says, "When I am called a 'Eurocentric racist' I am offended in just the same way as when a young Mexican-American student is called a 'wetback.'"

1. How are the epithets similar in their implications?

2. How are they different?

3. In what ways are young and old equally vulnerable to derogatory language?

4. In what ways are young and old differently vulnerable?

Voice

"... it's really hard to choose to be friends with, I think, one group, and then still be accepted in the other, and try and play middle of the road, because if you're with one group, you feel kind of funny because of the other group, and if you're with the other group, you feel kind of funny, because you kind of feel like, you know."

(Asian-American student)

Thought Experiment

A CASE OF SIBLING RIVALRY

At College L much energy of administrators and junior faculty has gone into new programs to help ethnic minority students to feel more at home on campus and to help them succeed. College L now has well-designed mentoring programs, an expanded ethnic studies program, sensitivity training for staff, and a minority students' ombudsman. An older faculty member says, "Maybe it's just because I am getting old, but the White students' behavior seems more sullen and more silly than I remember." A White woman junior says, "It's like the experience of a first child when there is a new baby. We just don't get the kind of attention we took for granted."

1. Is it plausible that White students might react as "sibling rivals" on your campus?

2. If so, what might be done to assure White students that they belong just as much as before?

Voice

"You know this person from my high school was . . . telling me that his roommate the first week was freaking. He said, 'Wow, there are so many Black people on campus.' This guy from my high school, he said, 'No there are not, you should have gone to high school with me.' About 25 percent of our school was, I would say, Black, and he said it was really odd for him because all of a sudden there were a lot of Asians and there weren't that many Blacks and there weren't that many Chicano people. . . . I guess how you perceive it depends upon where you are coming from."

(Asian student)

Reassessment of the values of multiple identifications is an ongoing part of student development. Such reassessment is by no means confined to students one of whose identifications is with an ethnic minority. Many Anglo students cannot comfortably see themselves as belonging to any ethnic culture that they can affirm without being regarded by themselves and others as racist, elitist, or insensitive. There are also some students of mixed-ethnic parentage who reject one or the other (or both) of their ethnic identifications.

Diversity on campus often marks an abrupt change in the context in which the individual student takes up development issues. A large proportion of today's students have grown up in neighborhoods where they were members of an overwhelming ethnic majority. In their high schools there were finely calibrated distinctions—as between "social" students and "nerds"—but often no important distinctions of race or ethnic culture among their perceived peers. On arriving at an ethnically diverse college campus, members of every group are likely to find their group's percentage of the student body much smaller than in their high schools. Students find themselves identified ethnically, and it becomes a task of immediate urgency to rethink their previous self-identification.

If all of this sounds complicated, it is. In the end, if you want to understand an individual student, there is no substitute for developing a relationship with *that* individual, a relationship which itself will have enough dimensions for the expression of who *that* student is and what *that* student is going through. If a faculty or staff member has no opportunity to develop such a relationship, and if there is cause for anxiety about where the process of a student's self-definition seems to be taking him or her, it is time for that person to find someone whose training, life experience, or both can supplement his or her own experience. A faculty or staff member of the same ethnicity as the student can sometimes provide crucial insights.

It is difficult for a college or university as an organization to know how individual students are dealing with a multiethnic context and to respond appropriately. Indeed, it has probably become more difficult. The decline of *in loco parentis*, and a specialization of contacts with students, especially in large institutions, work against any comprehensive view of the circumstances and developmental tasks of an individual student of the kind that college teachers once often had. The professor who notes a decline in a student's performance is unlikely to know, without making a special effort, whether the situation in the student's residence hall has changed, whether events have occurred that have undermined the student's self-confidence, whether the student's career horizon has expanded or contracted. Those who deal with these other aspects of the student's development—in sports, social groups, residence halls, and counseling centers—are unlikely to have much knowledge of his or her academic progress. When issues arise around any of these topics, no one person is in a very good position to know just how these aspects may interrelate with one another and with the student's developing sense of self, including ethnic identity. Colleges can usefully think about building new channels of communication to remedy these discontinuities in monitoring student development, as well as ways of assessing the campus climate in which this development takes place.

The surrender of *in loco parentis* and the greater specialization of student contacts may easily lead to a new or greater intolerance of what is, on its face, unattractive or self-destructive in student behavior, regardless of ethnicity. In more intimate academic settings, administration and faculty have in the past often been willing to accept a good deal of such behavior (even while trying to control and limit it) on the premise that what was objectionable was somehow linked with what was promising in students. Thus, a good deal of mildly antisocial behavior was put down to "blowing off steam," compensated for by serious academic effort. There may now be less forbearance of this kind on many campuses but just as much need for acceptance of the twists and turns of growing up. Lacking this acceptance, and given the feelings of unfamiliarity and inad-

Thought Experiment

A CASE IN STUDENT AID POLICY

College M is a small, moderately expensive liberal arts college. In order to recruit more African-American and Chicano students, the college has offered full need scholarships to 50 such students, but only for the freshman year. Other freshmen are angry because they are expected to take out loans for the first $2,500 of their financial need. For their part, the new African-American and Chicano students say the college has a "bait and switch" policy, since they will be expected to borrow in subsequent years. The following alternatives are suggested by the student aid administrator:

- Continue the present policy, as the most cost-effective way to recruit more African-American and Chicano students.

- Continue the present policy, but make a major effort to find or create enough well-paying jobs for students, so that they all can be offered the alternative of earning rather than borrowing the first $2,500 of need.

- Treat African-American and Chicano freshmen just like other freshmen, except guarantee African-American and Chicano students that they will not have to borrow more than $10,000 throughout the time they receive a bachelor's degree.

1. Which is the best alternative?

2. What financial considerations enter into decisions of low-income members of different ethnic groups about attending your institution?

3. Are these considerations different among different ethnic groups? How would you find out?

A CASE OF AUSTERITY

Small College N wants to take actions to assure students from underrepresented ethnic groups that they are welcome, that their success is important to the college, and that their voices will be heard and respected. Unfortunately, the budget of the institution is extremely tight. Compile a list of things a small college could do, each of which would cost less than $10,000.

Large University O is in comparable financial straits. Compile a list of things it could do, each of which would cost less than $50,000.

equacy faculty may feel in dealing with ethnic minority students, there may be a tendency to create distance between faculty and students and a general "uptightness."

Developmental theory offers a number of ideas for connecting what students do in a variety of settings and phases of maturation. These ideas may be especially useful in attempting to interpret both the behavior and attitudes of ethnic minority students and also the responses of majority students to greater ethnic diversity on campus. Stripped of most theoretical constructs, these are some of the phenomena frequently noted among traditional college-age students in general:

1. openness to new ideas, often evidenced by quickness in grasping concepts at the edge of a field

2. a wish to belong to recognizable groups whose participants demonstrate solidarity and conformity—often alternating with a sense of acute isolation

3. regression, apparent as a temporary loss of skills, mastery, and mature attitudes

4. high spirits, sometimes alternating with depression, reflected in tasks seeming harder than usual, pessimism, and preoccupation with bodily well-being or lack of it

5. judgmental moral standards, sometimes alternating with lapses in moral control and breakdowns in the link between moral standards and self-esteem

6. highly rationalized critiques of adults and the adult world, combined sometimes with a feeling that the adult world is unreal and sometimes with an intense wish to be part of that world

7. attitudes, practices, and involvements that represent experiments with self-perception, often abandoned without apparent trace

8. reluctance to sever ties with family or other environments perceived as nurturing at the same time that such ties are considered irksome

It may well be that much behavior that seems new in both minority and Anglo students exemplifies such phenomena in some way—with variations and shadings, of course. If what is seen makes sense in one of these ways, this may reduce any sense of pessimism and helplessness about intergroup relations and student outcomes. It may also induce more tolerance. If similar phenomena in other guises have been accepted and worked with in the past, they need not be viewed with alarm or anger as students of different ethnicities interact on today's campuses. Before alienation is put down to ethnicity, it needs to be remembered that *all* late adolescents may experience alienation. Before it is decided who belongs on campus and where they belong, it needs to be remembered that *all* late adolescents are engaged in internal debates about belonging or not belonging. Being offered constructive ways to belong is important to a positive educational outcome of these debates. Neither what is liked nor disliked about late adolescents is color-coded. All students can be serious at times, frivolous at times, easily discouraged or overconfident, generous or narrow in their loyalties.

Neither what is liked nor disliked about late adolescents is color-coded.

Even before students appear on campus, a college or university can begin to promote constructive outcomes to the processes of student development. A college or university campus can seem a very puzzling and forbidding place to *any* first-generation student, whether a member of an ethnic minority or not. How higher education connects with the opportunities of adulthood can be quite unclear. The challenge of catching up academically with students who have had better high school preparation may be intimidating. Outreach efforts, contacts with role models, and well-informed recruiters can help. So can campus-orientation visits, with time spent in classrooms and residence halls. Skills assessment and special instruction that conveys convincingly that people just like the student can, and are, succeeding academically can overcome both real and imagined obstacles to such success. A first-generation student, prepared to participate in campus life by such a "bridge program," can have the confidence needed to marshal energies, sort out competing claims on them, and succeed academically. Bridge programs have been tried in so many variations and on so many differing campuses that one of the more certain things known about ethnic diversity in higher education is that bridge programs *do* work.

Bridge programs have been tried in so many variations and on so many differing campuses that one of the more certain things known about ethnic diversity in higher education is that bridge programs do work.

Much of the foregoing assumes that the focus of interest in student development is the young student of traditional college-going age. As more and more students are older, other stages of development need to be considered as well. There never has been an *in loco parentis* responsibility toward older students; most live off-campus, out of sight most of the time. Many are preoccupied (and supported) by family and workplace relationships outside the university's jurisdiction and, ordinarily, beyond its concern as well. It should not be forgotten, however, that returning to

Thought Experiment

A CASE OF AN OLDER STUDENT

College P requires all undergraduates to take an American cultures course. An older African-American woman student is pursuing a degree to become a pharmacist. She protests the requirement:

"I work as a sales clerk full time. I can barely find the time to take the courses I really need and study for good grades in those courses. I don't need this 'cultures' course. I have lived diversity all my life. At the store I serve all kinds of people, including some who speak little English. I do it well. What would I gain from this cultures course?"

1. What might she gain?

2. What might she contribute?

3. How might a course in multiculturalism for working adults be different from one for younger students?

education after some years marks an important turning point in an older student's life, even if the purpose is a practical one of career advancement. Being a student may acquire many additional meanings as a result. It can release new energy and competence but also new anxieties. It may trigger much rethinking of one's own identity and fundamental commitments. All of this may be even more important for students from disadvantaged backgrounds, regardless of ethnicity, if they feel that a chance for higher education was denied them when they were younger, whether by poverty, lack of a high school diploma, or a sense that the available colleges and universities were hostile and forbidding places.

REFERENCES AND RESOURCES

General

Astin, A. W. *What Matters in College? Four Critical Years Revisited.* San Francisco, CA: Jossey-Bass, 1993.

Astone, B., and Nunez-Wormack, E. *Pursuing Diversity: Recruiting Minority College Students.* ASHE-ERIC Higher Education Report 1990, no. 7. Washington, DC: School of Education and Human Development, George Washington University, 1990. ED 333 857.

Bennett, C., and Okinaka, A. M. "Factors Related to Persistence among Asian, Black, Hispanic and White Undergraduates at a Predominantly White University: Comparison between First and Fourth Year Cohorts." *The Urban Review* 22(1) (1990): 33+.

Butler, J. E., and Walter, J. C., eds. *Transforming the Curriculum.* Albany, NY: State University of New York Press, 1991.

Lee, C. *Achieving Diversity: Issues in the Recruitment and Retention of Underrepresented Racial/Ethnic Students in Higher Education: A Review of the Literature.* Alexandria, VA: National Association of College Admissions Counselors, 1991. ED 338 941. Available from: National Association of College Admissions Counselors, 1800 Diagonal Road, Suite 430, Alexandria, VA 22314.

Pascarella, E., and Terenzini, P. T. *How College Affects Students: Findings and Insights from Twenty Years of Research.* San Francisco, CA: Jossey-Bass, 1991.

Phinney, J. S. "Stages of Ethnic Identity Development in Minority Group Adolescents." *Journal of Early Adolescence* 9(1-2) (1989).

Smith, D. G. *The Challenge of Diversity: Involvement or Alienation in the Academy?* ASHE-ERIC Higher Education Report 1989, no. 5. Washington, DC: School of Education and Human Development, George Washington University, 1989.

Wright, D. J., ed. *Responding to the Needs of Today's Minority Students.* New Directions for Student Services, no. 38. San Francisco, CA: Jossey-Bass, c1987.

African Americans

Astin, A. W. *The Black Undergraduate: Current Status and Trends in the Characteristics of Freshmen.* Los Angeles, CA: Higher Education Research Institute, Graduate School of Education, University of California, Los Angeles, [1990].

Stikes, C. S., *Black Students in Higher Education.* Carbondale, IL: Southern Illinois University Press, c1984.

Asian/Pacific Americans

Change 21(6) (Nov./Dec. 1989) (Special issue: "Asians and Pacific Americans: Behind the Myths").

Garner, B. "Southeast Asian Culture and the Classroom Climate." *College Teaching* 37 (1989): 127–30.

Nagasawa, R., and Espinosa, D. J. "Educational Achievement and the Adaptive Strategy of Asian American College Students: Facts, Theory, and Hypotheses." *Journal of College Student Development* 33(2) (Mar. 1992): 137–42.

Chicanos/Latinos

Change 20(3) (May/June 1988) (Special issue: "Hispanics and the Academy").

Olivas, M. A., ed. *Latino College Students.* New York, NY: Teachers College Press, c1986.

Native Americans

Benjamin, D. P., and Chambers, S. L. *Native American Persistence in Higher Education: Toward a Competency Model.* Paper presented at the 29th annual forum of the Association for Institutional Research, Baltimore, MD, April 30–May 3, 1989. 1989 ED 308 778.

Change 23(2) (Mar./Apr. 1991) (Special issue: "American Indians in Higher Education").

6

THE FACULTY ROLE

CASE

SYLVAN UNIVERSITY

The circumstances of ethnic minority faculty are reviewed in the context of a university's concern about what has caused a group of minority assistant professors to take other positions.

Sylvan University had been proud of its success in attracting minority faculty. It had not done as well as it would have liked, but it was satisfied that it was doing better than most other Ph.D.-granting institutions, public or private, in its region. It was particularly proud of the group of six Hispanic, Asian, and African-American tenure-track assistant professors it had recruited three years ago. Their presence had, collectively, given a new momentum to the university's diversity efforts. They were visible, respected, and well liked by their colleagues. The director of the admissions office noted that it seemed to be easier lately to recruit ethnic minority students, and she wondered whether Sylvan was getting positive recognition for its diversity efforts among off-campus constituencies.

Individually as well as collectively, the six faculty members had made some important contributions:

- A Chicano assistant professor of economics had done a study of past efforts to create common markets in Latin America that had earned him (and the university) recognition in the national debate about trade policy. He also served on the committee that had oversight of all Sylvan's endowed graduate fellowships.

- A Vietnamese assistant professor of French had given a course on colonial and post-colonial influences on the literature of Southeast Asia. She had been given a joint appointment in the Center for Comparative Literature, helping to revive general faculty interest in the work of the center.

- An African-American professor of history had served on two search committees and also the faculty senate committee on undergraduate programs. He had given a remarkable series of lectures on pre-1789 slavery that he was preparing to publish as a book.

- A Hispanic assistant professor of sociology was doing exciting fieldwork on the different roles of women in ghetto and barrio cultures. She had also helped design a study of campus climate at the request of the executive vice-president.

- An African-American assistant professor of engineering was doing important materials research and had been indispensable in recruiting students for the bridge program of the school of engineering.

- A Japanese-American assistant professor in the school of education was constructing a data base for a reanalysis of the predictive value of elementary school achievement tests. He also served on the campuswide committee that served as a court of appeal in discipline cases.

The contributions of the six had been such that it came as a shock when five of them resigned, effective the end of the current academic year. The materials engineer had accepted a position in a high-tech company. The economist had accepted an offer to be a senior fellow at a well-known think tank. The other three accepted academic appointments elsewhere, terms undisclosed. In each case, departmental persuasions and inducements to stay had failed to change the faculty member's mind.

The university at once took steps to replace the five. Three of the five had been hired originally under Sylvan's "target of opportunity" program, and the three slots were made available on the same basis immediately.

The African-American chair of the diversity committee of the faculty senate thought these steps insufficient and made an appointment with the vice-president for academic affairs.

"I'm discouraged," he said, "but I'm not mad at anybody. I just think we need to put our heads together and figure out whether we have only created a revolving door for minority faculty appointments."

Together the chair and the vice-president put together a list of hypotheses that might explain the resignations:

1. The five assistant professors had just been too good, so that other institutions had been eager to outbid Sylvan.

2. They had simply been overworked, especially by being asked to serve on so many committees.

3. They perhaps needed more support and encouragement for their research.

4. The university had perhaps put the six too often on display, a role about which they were probably ambivalent at best.

5. They perhaps had anxieties about whether they would achieve tenure at Sylvan.

6. There could be aspects of campus climate that made Sylvan less comfortable for the five than for the chair and the vice-president.

> *Are there additional possible explanations for Sylvan's problem in keeping minority faculty that it should consider?*

The chair and the vice-president then made a list of some things Sylvan might do to prevent "revolving door" losses in future:

1. Be prepared to make counteroffers *fast* and make sure department chairs know that the necessary funding discretion is available and is there to be used.

2. Allow minority hires more time before the tenure decision.

3. Give more weight to service assignments, including committee work, in the tenure decision.

4. Make it explicit that department chairs should help minority hires to find funding and other research support, and designate a university fund to provide support of last resort.

Are there additional actions that Sylvan should consider in dealing with its problem?

As the chair and the vice-president reviewed the lists they had made, they were both struck by the same thought, and at almost the same moment: Why not ask the sixth assistant professor who had *not* resigned what *she* thought? The sixth was the assistant professor of sociology.

When she joined them in the coffee room of the faculty club, she took her time to go over both lists.

"I'm sorry to be slow to respond," she finally said, "but the revolving door *is* a complicated thing. All your hypotheses are partial explanations, and all your proposals might help in one way or another, if implemented in a way that would not be condescending. But I can't say that any one hypothesis or proposal would be critical in all cases. I simply don't know.

"I also think there are a couple things you may be overlooking. One is that you tend to focus on the numbers. Six good appointments may have seemed to you like some kind of critical mass, enough to get the whole university moving. But, remember, each of these people has experienced the university as an individual, more or less isolated in the world of his or her own department, among departmental colleagues who are almost all White. What looked to you like a solid phalanx of minorities wasn't so at all to these five faculty members, or to me for that matter. Maybe it would have helped a good deal if there had been at least two or three minority-group members in *each* of those departments.

What mechanisms exist at your institution for faculty to talk honestly about their satisfaction and dissatisfaction and to take action when and where it is needed?

"The second thing you may be overlooking is, in a way, an extension of the first. The university has been so proud of the members of this group, so delighted with their contributions. Perhaps you are making the mistake of assuming that because *you* were so happy, *they* were happy too. It doesn't necessarily follow. I think we need better ways of finding out whether they were happy or not, and, if not, why not."

"That's extremely useful," said the vice-president, "but it brings up an inevitable question: why did *you* stay? I happen to know about some of your other offers."

"Well, again, it was two things," she responded. "First, and personal to me, was my involvement in the campus climate study. That brought me into contact with lots of people, faculty and students. I found I cared about them and about the community we all belong to. I guess I acquired a sense of the real potential for collegiality here. I certainly felt overworked during the study, but it also had the effect of giving me roots here.

What are some difficulties minority faculty at your institution have in being comfortable and productive?

"The other thing is that I have had appointments now at three universities, and I know the grass is *not* that much greener anywhere else. Wherever I am, I am going to have the same life of overwork, of sometimes being treated as a trophy, of building bridges and networks from scratch. In short, I am going to be leading the life of a minority woman academic in the real world. It's a useful life, and, on balance, I like it. And, if somewhere, why not here?"

DILEMMA

MIDWESTERN UNIVERSITY

Affirmative action in faculty hiring is a topic that brings out deeply held and opposed convictions. The context of this dilemma is an actual hiring decision.

The following are excerpts from the diary of a participant in an affirmative action search and comments from the faculty member actually hired.* The case is *not* fictitious, but the names of people and institutions are.

The Search Committee Member:

SEPTEMBER 23, 1989. The first faculty meeting of the term for the Department of English at Midwestern University. One of our assistant professors was denied tenure last year, and given the financial constraints on the university, we were anxious to find out whether we would be able to replace him. The chair of the department told us the following: "The dean has authorized a search at the assistant professor level for a 'minority' candidate."

Instantly the questions began. "What if we make a good-faith search and fail to come up with a suitable minority candidate? Can we then hire a non-minority candidate?" "Does the search include women or just ethnic minorities?" "What counts as a minority?"

Many of us, myself included, felt at this point that it would be good if we could find a suitable minority candidate but that we were not prepared to make any concessions about quality. Others were prepared to lower standards, on the grounds either that the traditional standards were biased toward "masculine," "European" criteria or that it was more important to provide a minority "role model" than to keep the same standards.

OCTOBER 15, 1989. We now had answers to some of the questions our chairman had taken to the dean. Blacks, "Hispanic-surnamed" persons, and Native Americans counted as minorities; East Indians and Asians did not. Thus, the first absurdity emerged. Someone born in Argentina to a Jewish family named Mendoza would count. A "boat person" from Vietnam would not.

---

*Excerpted and reprinted with permission from *Lingua Franca: The Review of Academic Life,* published in New York, April 1991 and August 1991.

NOVEMBER 10, 1989. (L)ooking day after day at applications from hopeful Ph.D.'s, I began to develop moral qualms. Basically, I was screening them for indications of race, not scholarship. It was as simple as the two piles of applications on my desk: one for minority candidates, another for non-minorities.

My equivocal moral position soon took on a more personal cast. A candidate at another school where I had been a visiting professor called me to inquire about the job. While he was otherwise quite promising, I knew that he really did not stand a chance of even getting an interview. How much of the situation ought I to reveal?

NOVEMBER 15, 1989. The search committee began to make a short list of candidates to invite for interviews at our annual association conference. Given the time and faculty available, we figured we could interview fourteen people, but it was clear that we didn't have fourteen potential minority interviewees. In fact, we had about twenty minority applications in all, about half of whom were just not qualified. We decided on four people to be interviewed, all Blacks, as it turned out, and none from this year's crop of Ph.D.'s. Rather, they were faculty members in tenure-track jobs. If we hired, we were going to be raiding other institutions.

DECEMBER 28–30, 1989. Nobody who hasn't sat in a stuffy hotel room for nine hours a day of job interviews can fully appreciate the horror of it all. I am not sure whether it is worse for the faculty or for the candidates. They, after all, get to talk about their work. We have to listen to nine mini-lectures a day. After the first few interviews, the attention lags. Virtually everybody was worse in person than on paper, which was inevitable, given the implausibility of their letters of recommendation: Every applicant was the "best in years." (This was true, in one professor's letter, for each of three candidates he was recommending.)

One candidate, however, the man from (Arctic University), actually proved more lively, more acute, and wittier than his letters suggested. He displayed a wide range of learning and an analytical mind, impressing the entire committee. Of course, we now had to read his work in more detail and he had to come give a paper to the department, but so far, so good. In addition, two other minority candidates were possibilities. Neither had done particularly well at the interview, but they both seemed to be good teachers and their letters were impressive. Among the non-minorities there were also two or three strong candidates.

That same day, one of the non-minority candidates we had interviewed, an extremely promising young professor from a major graduate department, cornered me in the hall. He was currently in an unhappy academic position that left him little time for research, in spite of which he had just had a book published by Stanford University Press. He was desperate to get another position, and he knew we had nobody in his area of expertise

Have you encountered a similar lack of candor or apparent hypocrisy on your campus?

in our department. "How did I do? Do you think I will get an invitation to campus?" Following my policy of not revealing more than I had been explicitly asked, I told him that while he had done well in the interview, the department would make the decision about whom to invite to campus, we had various needs and priorities, blah, blah, blah. But I knew that when he got the standard rejection letter he would blame himself for not doing better in the interview, not getting that extra letter of recommendation. I don't know if he would have felt better if I had said, "You're not going to get an interview. You're White." But *I* would have.

JANUARY 12, 1990. A startling development. The dean was so impressed with two of the people on the short list that he has given us permission to hire both of them if we so choose. A freebie.

We go around the room and get everyone's impressions. It becomes clear that the first offer is non-controversial. Indeed it is unanimous: the man from (Arctic). He is in a field that we do not cover now. He is clearly highly qualified. He is not an American Black (he's a West Indian), but that's the dean's worry. What about the second offer? Here things turn slightly nasty (in an academic way). It becomes clear that people in his area do not think that he is good enough. They have read his work and do not think it original or well argued. But, the argument from the opposition goes, we can't be sure that he isn't good enough. Why not hire him and let the tenure process decide that issue? Meanwhile we have an extra member of the faculty. How can it hurt?

But others, the majority, see another scenario as more convincing. In six years this person will have a long publication list in respectable journals. He will have made the academic contacts to get good letters of recom-

Are the disagreeable aspects of an affirmative action search felt by the first professor inevitable? Could the process have been better structured?

mendation. He will have made himself useful around campus. At that point, given that he is Black, it will be impossible for the university to deny him tenure—no matter what the judgement of his peers. So if we think now that the person is unlikely to produce excellent work, we must not make the appointment in the first place. Ultimately, that is the decision of the department. Ironically, in this case the candidate's race worked against him. Had he been White, many would have been willing to give him the benefit of the doubt, to give him the benefit of a trial period. But political realities made that impossible. It's also true that had he been White, he would not have made it to the interview stage.

NOVEMBER 1, 1990. Now that it's all over, what is my view of how affirmative action works in the university context? It certainly does not conform to the picture painted by the opponents of "quotas". No unqualified individual was forced upon a department against its better judgement, at the cost of passing up much better qualified non-minority candidates. Nor is it the case that the department had "internalized" the process so that, without being forced to, it voluntarily lowered its standards as a means to a good end. On the other hand, I do think that we were lucky: The outcome easily could have been worse. If we had been faced with the choice of the number-two candidate and a dean who said it was that person or the position goes back to the college, what would the department have done?

Had this been a color-blind competition, our winning candidate would almost certainly not have made it to the interviewing stage, where his talents were able to show. He was not from a major graduate department, his letters were not from major figures, and he was not teaching in a major department. These factors would have led to his being lost in the shuffle of nearly 300 applications. His being Black got him an interview.

In fact, since the candidate did not come from a major department, and since his letters of recommendation were not from important people in his area, many of us worried that we had made a wrong decision even after he was hired.

The Successful Candidate:

(The following are excerpts from the reflections of the candidate actually hired in this case, upon reading the diary excerpted above.)

. . . I hope that my own story will help illustrate . . . the failure of "Midwestern" University to reflect on the inherent biases of its procedures for evaluating minority candidates.

In a sense, my case is instructive precisely because of its atypicality. I had none of the handicaps with which the average Black American must struggle. As the son of a university professor in the Caribbean, I grew up on a university campus in my native country and attended an elite high school. As a member of a privileged class, I suffered none of the psychic wounding and destruction of self-confidence that systematic racism often causes. . .

I did my graduate work in Canada . . . because the schools were relatively cheap there. (From the diary I discovered that) in the American scheme of things (Arctic's) program just did not rank very high. This meant that, unbeknown to me and largely for financial reasons, I was already disadvantaged in the U.S. job market. And I hadn't even had to face the kinds of hurdles most Black Americans must surmount. . . .

(The Midwestern) department routinely uses the quality of the graduate school as a de facto filter. But how many talented Black students would have the resources to get into the schools on (the) preferred list? Since even getting into these schools requires surviving a whole pyramid of "screenings," mostly of a nonacademic kind, the uncritical application of this final filter is a de facto endorsement of a systematically biased status quo. . . .

Similar points can be made about the absence of big names on my CV (another revelation, this: So much for the standing of my Canadian referees!). If one has not been able to attend one of the top schools in the first place, how is one supposed to make contact with those rarefied circles?

My discipline is one in which the under-representation of Blacks is so extreme by comparison with other branches of the academy that it has become the subject of ongoing discussion in the profession's newsletter. It is an under-representation sustained less by overt racism than by subtle networks of ethnicity, whole hidden structures of personal contacts. This is not a conspiracy theory but the truism that people in the same profession tend to socialize together, and that to a significant extent in this country, their socializing continues to be along racial lines. And this is bound to affect crucial decisions about whom to interview and hire, whom to solicit for letters of recommendation and other professional evaluations, whom to invite to conferences or to publish in journals. In their exclusivity, their reliance on who-knows-whom, these networks can also work against Whites. But through race and class disadvantage, Black academics will probably be handicapped to begin with in graduate school and in their profession, and psychically burdened by their isolation. For them, the ethnic character of these networks represents a further heightening of these barriers that is not faced by White academics. . . .

How would you assess the importance of "subtle networks of ethnicity" in circumscribing the pools of talent from which your institution selects faculty?

(The diarist) admits that without affirmative action, I would never have made the interview list. Yet, within the set of possibilities open to me, I had done what was necessary: gone to a good but affordable school, gotten strong letters of recommendation, and started publishing. But by (Midwestern) standards (Arctic) wasn't good enough, my letters weren't from big enough names, and my publications were presumably insufficient or irrelevant. Had the search been conducted on ostensibly nonracial grounds, I would still be at . . . (the first school that hired me) today. And if three years before, the dean at (that institution) had not put pressure on its department to conduct a minority search, and had there not been one individual in that department who insisted this recommendation be taken seriously, I would be out of the academy altogether. After graduating from (Arctic), I was unemployed in Canada for two years, and at the professional meeting where I got the offer (of my first academic position), I had decided that if nothing worked out there, it was time to cut my losses and try in midlife to change careers.

This needs some emphasis, since in a sense it is the whole point of my story: Despite all the advantages with which I began, despite the abilities that (the diarist) praises, it is only through affirmative action that I am a university professor today...

The department at Midwestern has been very good to me, and I expect to be happy here.

But I have no illusions about how I came to be here. When I visit Canada or the Caribbean and friends or former fellow students ask me how I made it, I have a standard answer:

"Ability, hard work, race, and luck—not 'not necessarily in that order' but necessarily not in that order."

All policies will have social costs, and I don't want to deny that occasional inequities may result from affirmative action. But the alternative is, it seems to me, to continue with a system that is not neutral but continues in diverse blatant and subtle ways to be stacked against racial minorities.

BACKGROUND ESSAY

A professor of English might say, "Diversity has made us all anthropologists." A professor of anthropology might counter, "Diversity has made us all humanists."

What such an exchange underlines is that diversity is both a powerful and attractive intellectual stimulus and also a new demand on faculty energies. These factors can cause faculty to feel either that they are intellectual pathmakers or that they are uncomfortably like novices in someone else's field—or both. The balance of factors may determine whether individual faculty contribute to a successful and exciting intellectual engagement with ethnic diversity or tend to resist change. Administration can seek to tip the balance with incentive programs, but the most powerful motivations will remain intellectual and academic,

---

Those who have seen the intellectual excitement of the new challenges (often because of circumstances in their personal histories) need to find ways to convey this excitement to others.

---

including opportunities for doing research and for finding new ways of conceptually engaging students. Those who have seen the intellectual excitement of the new challenges (often because of circumstances in their personal histories) need to find ways to convey this excitement to others. In many cases it will not be an easy task. Personal and intellectual example will often succeed where sermons fail.

Members of the different academic disciplines will inevitably see the tasks and opportunities of diversity differently. In some scientific fields, both research topics and methods may seem relatively unaffected, although even in these fields diversity may draw attention to opportunities to recruit new talent, to develop new teaching methods, or to develop new avenues for the application of findings. In professional fields, the impetus for engaging diversity is likely to be different, because standards and requirements may be seen as coming largely from outside the academy: from the profession itself, from licensing authorities, and from those who employ people with professional qualifications. In professional fields where ethnic minorities have been pervasively underrepresented, diversity requires that more minority professionals be trained and that *all* professionals learn to become more adept in serving an ever more diverse society.

Voice

"I have survived because I do two sets of research: one on Black women's issues, and one that is main-streamed within my profession. It is the only way I will have legitimacy when tenure time comes."

(Black woman faculty member)

In the academic social sciences and in the humanities, views of the challenges of diversity are likely to be different yet again. Choices about curriculum and research directions are much more autonomous and open to revision in these fields. For this reason, much of the most spirited discussion of disciplinary adaptation to diversity has occurred here. Much of the new scholarship envisions a more inclusive basis for developing standards of quality research. This scholarship contends that research that strives for the description and explanation of the psychological, sociological, political, or economic dynamics of particular communities can be as valid as research that strives from the outset for universalist explanation. This new scholarship argues that research directly motivated by concern for the amelioration of social conditions is as likely to contribute to intellectual progress as research motivated by the construction of the next step in an emerging theoretical model of a discipline. Before rejecting this view, everyone would do well to examine its arguments. Rather than simply assuming that the new intellectual currents are too parochial to be broadly significant intellectually, it is worth considering the possibility that biases in our own intellectual frameworks lead us in parochial ways to define what is parochial.

Because the academic disciplines differ, the character of the adaptation to diversity is bound to vary among departments and schools at the same institution. The idea that some schools and departments are "lagging" in dealing with diversity often reflects this kind of variation rather than a lack of motivation. Still, even highly comparable academic departments may differ in their ability and willingness to see their own appropriate tasks in an ethnically diverse college or university. Those who speak and act for a vision of what the institution as a whole wants to become need to be a pervasive influence transcending departmental differences.

Faculty have many roles in making a college or university a successful, diverse community. They are expected to exemplify respect for knowledge and the methodologies that validate knowledge. Importantly, they also participate in setting the institution's priorities. The centrality of

Voice

"And when all of the things that seem most important to me are questioned so radically, when all of the things I care most about are attacked as being the accidental or evil by-products of some repressive colonial patriarchal mentality, then I'm attacked. And I've got to work this through by thinking and writing about it. . . . (A)fter the shaking of the cultural tree that is now going on, we'll find out what remains. And I always believe that quality will out, that if things are good, they'll survive."

(White faculty member)

Thought Experiment

ACADEMIC INFLUENCES

Department K at University Q has found the following influences important in choices of research direction made by graduate students and faculty, in this order:

- the interests of senior faculty
- new breakthroughs in methodology
- peer interests
- the ethnicity of the student or faculty member
- facilities, library holdings, and support for research
- targeted fellowships, awards, and other incentives

1. Are these influences important in your department? In this order?

2. How would they affect research choices that engage diversity?

faculty contributions to diversity and the multiplicity of faculty roles can be depicted in a diagram:

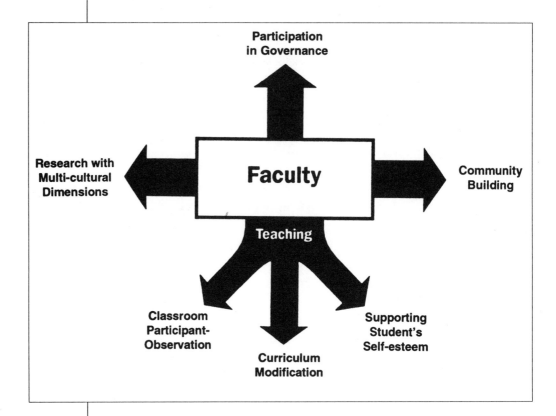

All of these faculty roles converge on teaching. Adapting teaching methods and styles to new contexts of diversity will be a major claim on the energies of faculty in the next decade. Faculty will need to find ways to engage the intellectual curiosity of students from a great variety of backgrounds. For the most part, it will have to be White faculty who do this. For the next 20 years, at most institutions, the percentage of faculty who are White will be far higher than the percentage of students who are White. Such faculty will need to make connections between academic topics and what is important in the lives of students whose experience of life such faculty often understand very imperfectly.

It is important not to underestimate the difficulty of these tasks, but it is also important not to underestimate faculty resources for accomplishing them. The adaptation and improvement of the intellectual content of their teaching is a *normal* role of faculty. Faculty have always had to find ways to communicate new findings, new methodologies, and new technologies. Faculty have always had the task of overcoming boredom and making learning

Thought Experiment

CHALLENGING THE TEXTBOOK

A professor notes that ethnic minority students in her class rarely challenge what is said in the textbook. How well might the following tactics work in encouraging wider critical thinking about the textbook?

1. Reward critical students with special praise.

2. Ask the students who are uncritical what is wrong with specific statements in the textbook.

3. Assign additional readings at odds with the text.

4. Use short written assignments to elicit criticism in lieu of classroom discussion.

5. Ask students to chair the discussion in rotation.

more exciting. Some faculty have talents that enable them to do this better than others, but all except the most burnt-out are trying to do it every day. Faculty must get the credit for such old innovations as adapting the case-study method to a variety of disciplines and for such new ones as teaching writing throughout the curriculum and making mathematics less intimidating. And it is faculty who are constantly conducting small-scale curriculum experiments by trying one text rather than another in order to find those that will best communicate important perspectives and engage their students intellectually.

> ### *The adaptation and improvement of the intellectual content of their teaching is a* normal *role of faculty.*

Faculty members tend to be conscious of and articulate and innovative about these issues of pedagogy, but they may be less so in dealing with the details of student-teacher contact in a diverse classroom. The quality of these contacts takes on additional importance because a good many late adolescents see professors as extremely mysterious and powerful and because so many more students are "nontraditional" students who spend little time on campus when not attending class.

There is nothing new about the sensitivity of students to the nuances of faculty behavior, but differences in ethnic culture can heighten the effect of these nuances. The exact phrase a professor uses in announcing office hours may be over- and misinterpreted to mean that the professor does not want to be disturbed. A smile of welcome toward a White student the professor ran across last year may be seen as a preference for White students. Any discernible pattern in which students are asked questions in class may be seen as carrying definite messages of high or low expectations.

Some problems springing from sensitivities like these can and should be anticipated and guarded against. To minimize the harm that cannot be anticipated, two things are helpful. First, a faculty member can make a habit of showing a level of interest and responsiveness that affirms concern for the development of each student. Second, when despite such a general policy a student is hurt by a particular incident, the faculty member can usually move promptly to make a healing explanation.

For example, suppose a Black freshman in a hurry bursts in on her faculty advisor without much ceremony. The professor, who is talking with another student, says, "Around here, we knock before entering." The Black student retreats, feeling that old wounds have been reopened. The cross-currents in such an incident say a good deal about the stresses of faculty and students coming to terms with diversity on an American campus. The professor thinks that he is pointing out a minor point of good manners that members of the campus community observe as part of living together. It is *because* he regards the Black freshman as a new, but fully responsible member of the community that a mild reproof seems to him appropriate. To say nothing (or to be elaborately tactful) would seem to him patronizing, a way of saying that the student does not quite belong. But to the student it may sound as though an inadequacy of her background is being asserted, that she does not really belong "around here."

Both the professor and the student want to validate the student's participation and make it fully productive, but what the one does to achieve this seems to the other to withdraw any such validation. The professor feels that inclusion of the minority student is perfectly consistent with the institution's being authoritative about behavior, curriculum, and intellectual standards. Indeed, that inclusion *requires* such an authoritative stance. But the student comes with a very different personal and community history that sees such authority as either reimposing subordination or undercutting her hard-

Voice

"Right now I'm dealing with a professor, and I'm having a lot of racial problems with him. . . . Just recently in class, I asked a simple question about an experiment that we were doing, and he implied that I was stupid for asking the question. From talking to other Black students who have had him in the past, they say that they've had problems and they've confronted him. His comment to me and them is, 'Don't take it personally.' Well, what am I supposed to do? I don't care how much you don't like me, the main reason I'm in that classroom is to learn."

(Black student)

earned self-esteem. The effect is worse, not better, because she cannot be entirely sure whether the aggression she perceives is against her as a member of a minority group or as a woman. It is hard to mobilize one's inner resources against ambiguous threats. For all of these reasons, it can make an enormous difference if the faculty member is attuned enough to student feelings to later remark, "I hope I didn't sound unfriendly before, but you really should knock first, because sometimes my office needs to be as private as we would like it to be in the rooms where we live."

The diffidence of both teachers and students can provide much material for misunderstanding. To avoid being assertive in order to avoid being perceived as aggressive can entail failing to get an important message or expectation across from either side, the student's or the faculty member's. A professor's efforts to avoid hurting a student's feelings through a failure to provide honest evaluation is patronizing. On the other hand, a professor may be exasperated when a student does not ask for timely help because of shyness. A particular problem causing shyness for some students, including some very competent ones, is an accent or difficulty with the convolutions of spoken English syntax. Such students are often convinced that fellow students and faculty think they are stupid because of their way of speaking, even if their peers and professors think nothing of the kind.

To avoid being assertive in order to avoid being perceived as aggressive can entail failing to get an important message or expectation across from either side, the student's or the faculty member's.

Taking note of all the sensitivities and possible sources of misunderstanding in a diverse classroom and then teaching responsively may seem to add greatly to the already difficult tasks of teaching. That may be so, at least initially. One approach is to ask students themselves to share the task. An open discussion, early in a course, of how everyone is expected to participate and how they can help one another to do so accomplishes some of this sharing. The faculty member can say how much he or she appreciates it when students draw one another out. Assignments can be structured so that each student will sooner or later be the obvious person to lead a discussion. The instructor can break up patterns of seating that make some students feel like nonparticipants and explain to the class why he or she is doing so. Collaborative projects can be designed to make clear that each student is an essential member of a team. Team assignments may need to be a serious part of each student's grade if there is to be strong enough motivation to overcome barriers among team members.

If a teacher has found effective ways to engage students intellectually and has also found relatively static-free modes of classroom communication, there are likely to be some students who will be willing and able to see the teacher as a role model. Perhaps very few faculty members deliberately set about achieving this result, but its value can be enormous in terms of the personal and intellectual growth of students and in terms of building bridges between genders, races, and generations. Even a short list of what students can seek in such relationships makes clear their importance for student growth. A faculty member can be a model of

> ### Voice
> "My teachers, all but one, don't know how to treat me. They are always slightly surprised when I ask a probing or thoughtful question."
> (Black woman student)

- impartial judgment
- investigative curiosity
- participant observation
- thoroughness and tenacity
- the courage to be original
- clarity of expression
- intelligent and practical caring for other people

Although it is implausible to expect faculty members to be paragons in all these respects all of the time, it is worth considering how much stands to be lost if any student is prevented from making any of these connections by an inadvertent insensitivity on the part of a faculty member.

The presence on campus of faculty who themselves are members of minority ethnic groups can be an enormous asset in making the adjustments *all* faculty will need and want to make. Their presence and full participation in campus affairs means opportunities to test ideas, to see alternative approaches in action, and to have feedback from students analyzed by someone who sees matters from a faculty point of view, yet based on a minority life experience. Making minority faculty appointments enables the institution to affirm in a visible way that it respects ethnic cultures, wants to include new energies and perspectives, and intends to create pathways to success for all students.

Thought Experiment

A CASE OF ETHNIC COMPLEXITY

Three out of four Hispanic professors who teach at College S are Latin American by birth.

1. Does this fact make the professors less representative of American-born Hispanic students?

2. What might be some of the complaints of Latino students about the situation? Which would be most persuasive?

3. Would you favor giving preference to American-born Hispanics in future hiring?

These advantages of faculty diversity, along with the rights of minority academics for equality of opportunity as individuals, are sufficient reasons for special efforts to recruit minority faculty. Minority faculty can serve as role models, but so can other faculty. Nor need it be argued that only the members of a particular ethnic group can understand that group's needs and culture. Obviously, membership in the group can often make investigations of such matters more timely and more productive of insight, but no monopoly claims need be asserted. As in many areas, making an exaggerated case can alienate support for a good and strong case rather than recruit more support for it.

Making minority faculty appointments enables the institution to affirm in a visible way that it respects ethnic cultures, wants to include new energies and perspectives, and intends to create pathways to success for all students.

Exaggeration is also prominent in arguments that the small numbers of minority Ph.D.'s coming out of "the pipeline" make the problems of minority recruitment insoluble. It is certainly true that, for some years anyway, the number of minority Ph.D.'s will not be proportional to minority numbers in the population at large or in most student bodies. But this need not be read as counsel of despair. The value of a minority presence on the faculty is not contingent on strict proportional representation. Further, the fact that there will be competition in hiring minority faculty can itself be read (and will be read by today's students) as an affirmation of the values of their inclusion. In this competition, it need not always be some other institution that wins. Colleges and universities are so varied that each can look closely for its own special advantages in the competition and expect to find some.

- The diverse character of the student body may be just what the prospective faculty member seeks.

- The colleagues a minority faculty member would work with may constitute a close and productive research group the recruit would like to join.

- Nearby libraries, laboratories, or universities can offer highly attractive research opportunities, and sometimes joint appointments.

- There may be very special opportunities for the recruit's spouse, in the institution or in the local area.

- The traditions (including the religious affiliation) of the college may be highly important to the recruit.

- The college may be close to the recruit's parents or offspring.

- A benefactor may be willing to invest in the recruit's specific line of research.

• The community may be just the kind of place where the recruit would like to bring up a family.

Not everyone can win all of the time in the effort to diversify the faculty, but no one need lose all of the time, either.

One approach that has been successful on a number of campuses in making the pipeline problem much more manageable is "target of opportunity" hiring. In many institutions, departments are organized to provide coverage of a number of subdisciplinary fields, and faculty members are expected to achieve national and international reputations for scholarly work and publication in their specific areas of specialization and expertise. The tendency is against hiring generalists, people with the "wrong" specializations, or faculty whose achievements mainly consist of outstanding teaching and service. Faculty search committees, chairs, deans, and other administrators jealously guard the recruitment priorities of departments. Taken together, these factors have the effect of narrowing the pool of prospective faculty hires far more than would appear to be indicated by statistics on the availability of eligible Ph.D.'s in a given field or discipline.

Not everyone can win all of the time in the effort to diversify the faculty, but no one need lose all of the time, either.

The target-of-opportunity strategy for dealing with this situation is based on setting aside specific funds for positions not initially designated by department or subdiscipline. The maximization of excellence in such cases is achieved through competition among departments for a limited pool of positions to be awarded to the departments that can produce the most academically convincing case for a proposed female or minority hire, whatever the candidate's specialization. Such target-of-opportunity programs can, in principle, contribute dramatically to the enhancement of faculty diversity while augmenting academic quality.

REFERENCES AND RESOURCES

Achieving Faculty Diversity: A Sourcebook of Ideas and Success Stories. Madison, WI: The University of Wisconsin System, 1988.

Adams, M., ed. *Promoting Diversity in College Classrooms: Innovative Responses for the Curriculum, Faculty, and Institutions.* New Directions for Teaching and Learning, no. 52. San Francisco, CA: Jossey-Bass, 1992.

Border, L. L. B., and Chism, N. V. N., eds. New Directions for Teaching and Learning, no. 49. *Teaching for Diversity.* San Francisco, CA: Jossey-Bass, 1992.

Claxton, C. S., and Murrell, P. H., eds. *Learning Styles: Implications for Improving Educational Practices.* ASHE-ERIC Higher Education Report, no. 4. Washington, DC: Association for the Study of Higher Education, 1987.

Cooper, R., and Smith, B. L. "Achieving a Diverse Faculty: Lessons from the Experience of The Evergreen State College." *AAHE-Bulletin* 42(2) (Oct. 1990):10–12.

Green, M. F., ed. *Minorities on Campus: A Handbook for Enhancing Diversity.* Washington, DC: American Council on Education, 1989.

Mickelson, R. A., and Oliver, M. L. "Making the Short List: Black Candidates and the Faculty Recruitment Process." In *The Racial Crisis in American Higher Education*, edited by Philip G. Altbach and Kofi Lomotey, 149–66. Albany, NY: State University of New York Press, c1991.

Moses, Y., and Higgins, P., eds. *Anthropology and Multicultural Education: Classroom Applications.* Athens, GA: University of Georgia, 1981. ED 231 690.

Nordquist, J. *The Multicultural Education Debate in the University: A Bibliography.* Santa Cruz, CA: Reference and Research Services, 1992.

Pluralism in the Professoriate: Strategies for Developing Faculty Diversity. Washington, DC: National Institute of Independent Colleges and Universities, 1991. ED 342 860.

The Role of Faculty in Multicultural Education. Los Angeles, CA: Prism/ Mount St. Mary's College.

Schoem, D., et al., eds. *Multicultural Teaching in the University.* Westport, CT: Praeger, c1993.

7

LEADERSHIP FOR DIVERSITY

CASE

WALDER UNIVERSITY

Campus leaders encounter some of the frustrations that can occur in making a multicultural curriculum a reality.

The new president of Walder University did not consider himself an expert on the topic of curriculum reform, nor had he been chosen as such an expert. His mandate from the trustees was, first and foremost, to do something about a troubling decline in undergraduate enrollments. Walder's tuition charges no doubt played a role in this decline, but the new president saw economics as only a part of the picture. He believed many parents and students were inclined to see their choice as between a small liberal arts college and a relatively low-tuition large public institution. To make Walder, a private university, a viable third option, Walder had to become a distinctive and intellectually exciting place. Thus, a very practical perspective led the president, non-expert though he was, to attach importance to curriculum reform.

The president said much of this to the provost, asking her what she thought about making curriculum reform a major priority. At Walder, it was to the provost that responsibility for implementing such an initiative would be delegated.

The provost was uncertain how to respond. On the one hand, she had seen the goals of liberal education gradually eclipsed at Walder over the years and would very much like to see that trend reversed. Equipping students to live in a diverse society was, to her mind, clearly one important such goal. Thus, in principle, she would like to be supportive.

However, the provost was concerned that the president know what he was getting into. He needed to know that his concerns about distinctiveness of mission and enrollments might largely be lost sight of in the process of hammering out curriculum reforms. Intellectually, diversity would be one theme among others in a reformed curriculum, but politically it would be absolutely central and possibly divisive. Gone were the days when an initiative at Walder could consist of a high-level committee, an eloquent report, and decorous negotiations among departments. There would be polarization and rhetorical violence. The provost asked herself, "Should I make clear how much energy the process will consume, and how thankless it could easily be? If I make these things clear, he might back off, but if I don't he will be unprepared for what may come."

The provost decided to state both sides of the case to the president, who thanked her and said, "Can we make this discussion a standard of candor

Given the chair's lack of enthusiasm, the provost was surprised how well the process went. To be sure, the first two meetings of the Senate committee on curriculum reform were dominated by speeches insisting on the apocalyptic

---

Some Interim Questions

At your institution are considerations about process as important as they are at Walder?

Do such process considerations reflect important academic values at your institution?

On your campus would it be important to consider trustee, student, and staff viewpoints at this stage as well as the faculty's?

---

urgency of doing what each speaker recommended and a very deliberate leisureliness in considering faults, large or small, in all other proposals.

However, the provost, who insisted she was present "only to get educated," thought she saw the outlines of a compromise proposal take shape. Existing distribution requirements could be replaced by a menu of courses under the general rubric of "American Cultures and Human Values." Students could be required to select three or four such courses in their first two years. Courses would be approved for inclusion in the menu only if they addressed methods of intellectual analysis and also the history and circumstances of more than one ethnic group. The criteria could be applied in such a way as to guarantee opportunities for participation by members of all three of the most interested faculty parties and to assure enough approvals so that students could, if they chose, avoid taking any course they would be likely to see as ideological indoctrination. There need be no set of approved texts, thus ducking the "canon" issue.

A proposal along these lines went forward, guided by the "peace making" members of the committee, but a price had to be paid—or, rather, several prices. One trustee became convinced that the proposal was the "thin end of the wedge" that would eventually damage the university irretrievably. The president could not convince him otherwise and regretted that he had probably lost the trustee's support on other issues.

The three most interested faculty constituencies insisted on additional criteria for course approval—respectively, a focus on issues of "race, class, and gender," an exact list of which ethnic groups counted, and a reference to "classics of Western civilization." The provost hoped that the students would not absorb similarly bureaucratic views of liberal education and diversity.

The students themselves also had their price: Their representatives insisted that the courses should be for credit, but on a pass/fail basis. They argued that such an untried curriculum should not put students' grade point averages at risk.

The compromise that was trickiest to negotiate was that with the ethnic studies centers. Their first demand was that teaching an approved course on the menu should automatically confer joint-appointment status in a traditional academic department. The provost was sure that such a commitment would result in opposition from the traditional departments that would instantly crush the entire plan. She offered half a loaf: Only the tenured head of each of the four centers would receive such a joint appointment. She felt she could manage that with the departments concerned.

The provost breathed a sigh of relief when the proposal was accepted by the committee subject to these provisos, and she congratulated herself on her astuteness as an academic politician. She reported to the president, "I think we have brought this off. You are going to have to find some money for it. And I don't like, any more than you do, all this distrust and negotiating for position. It defeats our purpose somewhat, I know. But it is the best we can do."

"I expect it is," the president replied, "but I have a feeling some of these compromises are going to come back to haunt us."

The president's forebodings were correct. Planning for the first semester in which the new courses were to be taught demonstrated how fragile some of the compromises were. A professor who had previously taught an interdisciplinary seminar in the evolution of moral concepts in Western civilization

---

Some Interim Questions

How important has negotiating skill become as an aspect of leadership on your campus? For dealing with diversity issues specifically?

Would the kinds of compromise in this case be acceptable on your campus? Would they be feasible?

---

offered to develop a new course on the evolution of moral teaching in families of varying ethnic origins. His course proposal made it clear that he intended to discuss only assimilated families of Jewish, Hispanic, and Chinese origin, starting with classic religious texts in these three traditions. A few militant faculty on the course approval committee were outraged, regarding the texts as patriarchal and authoritarian. Members of the committee from ethnic studies were furious also, believing that the course would assert the implicit premise that assimilation was a desirable goal for all ethnic groups. More traditional faculty on the committee abstained, being fairly sure that the moral concepts professor had deliberately designed his new course to outrage the other groups. The course was disapproved.

The moral concepts professor then prepared a statement for the full senate in which he said that the forces of political correctness had shown their intention to exercise exclusive control over the new curriculum, even at the cost of undermining substantive and procedural guidelines intended to protect academic freedom. He released his statement to the campus newspaper and to general circulation newspapers as well. Faculty took sides on the procedural issues, even faculty who had little interest in the general education and diversity program.

The president and provost felt betrayed. Both the moral concepts professor and the furious members of the other faculty groups had, in fact, been parties to the compromises that had enabled the new curriculum to go forward. All of them well understood that a good deal of forbearance in pressing their own positions was indispensable for the plan to work, and they had, in some cases explicitly, promised such forbearance. The president and provost also felt that the dispute had been framed in terms that left them powerless to demand that earlier promises be kept. They could not charge betrayal without opening the university's wounds even wider. Besides, senior administrators at Walder *never* expressed opinions or even concern about the choice of texts in particular courses. The president and provost were thus reduced to uttering platitudes about relying on the wisdom and goodwill of the faculty.

The Senate chair felt constrained in none of these ways. He felt now was the time to expend some of his capital, to save Walder from gridlock and ridicule. He examined closely the resolution that had endorsed the new curriculum and found that the full senate had not relinquished the right to review and reverse actions of the course approval committee. He had a series of conversations with leaders of the various senate factions, pointing out what each stood to lose if the curriculum reform had to be either abandoned or restrictively modified. He was all the more persuasive because his earlier skepticism was well known. His transparent interest was in the health and strength of the university as an academic community and in an effective faculty voice in its governance. He won approval from the full senate.

"Sometimes," he said afterwards, "what is needed is leadership in keeping an open mind and getting others to open up theirs."

Some Concluding Questions for Discussion

If the president, provost, and Senate chair at Walder "had it all to do over again," what better strategies could they have adopted?

How would you assess, on balance, the demands, risks, and rewards of leadership on diversity issues at your institution? For faculty, administrators, and student leaders?

DILEMMA

AN EXCHANGE OF ELECTRONIC MAIL

Two college presidents, Rebecca Arthur and Neil Jackson, review their thinking about making diversity a top priority for their administrations. The context is an exchange of messages via electronic mail.

Dear Neil:

I was much impressed by your call for presidential leadership on multiculturalism at the association's retreat. But my purpose in contacting you is not to congratulate you but to get your personal advice. When it comes to my stepping out in front on these issues—at this college at this time—then I'm not convinced. You may think I'm gutless or reactionary, but I just don't think I can take on the leadership role you have. Here are my reservations:

1. At the moment, this college doesn't care about diversity or multiculturalism. At the same time, this is not a racist institution. Although we have less than 10 percent minority enrollment, these students do reasonably well. I don't sense opposition to some increase in their numbers, but, except for a brief discussion about funds for minority scholarships, the board of trustees has not discussed diversity in the several years of my tenure. There is only somewhat more interest among faculty and students. By and large, they say that when they are in a more diverse environment, they will then figure out how to handle it. What I *do* hear about, especially from the board and the faculty, is money, buildings, equipment, visibility, and prestige. Frankly, those are the things I have concentrated on, and I don't see where multiculturalism fits in.

President Arthur is torn between being responsive to current priorities and taking an initiative on diversity. Is there such tension for leaders at your institution?

2. Even if I were to decide to exert some leadership on diversity, where would the active support come from? What I read about diversity suggests that faculty leadership and involvement would be critical. No way! We can't attract much faculty leadership on issues where they agree they should take a strong hand, such as general education requirements. I don't know of a single funding source for this college that wouldn't prefer to give money to some particular cause other than a diversity effort.

3. I fear, and others do too, what diversity would do to our sense of community on campus. Some of the more idealistic enthusiasts for diversity talk about building a "new community." But we've already got

a community! I'm not glad that our community is overwhelmingly White. But if we became more diverse, then I am afraid that we would see the growth of ethnic enclaves and separatism, not a community at all. Yes, we have had a few racial incidents on campus. But, in every case, we got our lawyers involved quickly and we have avoided both lawsuits and nasty publicity. The assertion is made by some that every college, at least in this part of the nation, will have to deal with diversity sooner or later, and that sooner is better than later. I don't see that.

> Is it true that, in dealing with diversity issues, sooner is better than later? Would the experience of your campus bear this out?

Please give me your reactions to all this, on a confidential basis.

Dear Becky:

Two years ago I had a conversation with another president in which he said much what you have said. I made all of the standard arguments you have already heard, and I finished by telling him, in effect, that he had a professional obligation to exert some leadership on behalf of diversity. After reflection, I won't try the same plea on you. Let me just list some of the things I have learned from my own experience and from listening to the experiences of others. This is not fancy social science research, but I do think there are some observations worth your hearing.

1. Several other presidents have told me that they wish they could "get through the diversity issue and on to their real jobs." This is a misreading of the situation. The change in the composition of our society is not a one-time problem to be solved but part of a changed reality that we will all spend the rest of our lives dealing with. This statement is hard to swallow, but it's true. I've also heard a kind of exasperated anger expressed: "Didn't we solve this problem in the sixties? What's the problem now?" But we didn't solve the problem in the "sixties." The anger, the injustice, the conflict is still out there. The question for us is what role we play in producing the leadership, of all colors, to deal with it.

2. It's hard for you to see why you should be dealing with diversity issues. But you already are. If you scratch beneath the surface, then you quickly discover that an institution's stance with respect to race, ethnicity, and gender is tied to choices you have made about institutional purpose, curriculum, criteria for hiring and promotion, allocation of resources for curricular changes, financial aid, student counseling, the nature of cultural and artistic events on campus, public relations, fund raising, and even physical facilities. Perhaps you don't recognize it, but your comments to me are saying, "We are now positioned as a somewhat elite, virtually all-White institution and we intend to continue that way." It sounds to me, and forgive me if I am wrong, that your campus is making a fundamental, strategic decision about its future in terms of the past.

President Jackson believes that a decision about investing leadership in diversity is an unavoidable decision about the future of a college or university. Do you agree?

3. The question that might be posed to the trustees, the faculty, the staff, the students, and the alumni is not so much the issue of diversity but the future of the institution in an environment that is rapidly becoming more diverse. I'd bet that there is a sizable number of faculty who would like to become part of that discussion. I doubt that any president can dictate or even foresee the outcome of such a discussion, but people in our position play a crucial role in framing it and getting it started. It is vital that such a discussion be grounded not in everybody's wish list of the things they'd like to keep them happy, but in the challenges that the institution should choose to face in the next decade.

4. How to get such a conversation started? I distrust cookbook answers to such an important question. One approach that has worked for me is to get together a dozen or so of the brightest thinkers and best human beings on campus, including some trustees and faculty, to think about the future of the institution, to put down their thoughts in a brief paper, and then all to go away on a retreat for a couple of days. Such a gathering might be undertaken with the understanding that whatever is discussed will be brought back to campus for many other groups to consider over a period of months. A few thoughtful people from other campuses might be helpful in both the initial and continuing discussions.

5. I expect you fear that a discussion of diversity issues would simply reproduce the same old ideological arguments. The media tends to play these discussions as a juicy conflict between sharp-tongued zealots on the left and right. Don't let the media control *your* debate! Instead focus on live, local issues specific to your campus. One helpful step can be a study of campus climate, done through focus groups, interviews, and/or survey questionnaires that turn people's attention to what your students, faculty, and staff actually think about the current state of community and diversity on your campus.

6. Some of your White students tell you that they'll figure out how to function with people from other racial and ethnic groups when life requires them to do so. That view makes as much sense to me as throwing people in the water to teach them how to swim. The ability to work with people from different traditions, life experiences, and beliefs tends to generalize the more you do it. I think the skills of veteran foreign service officers and even Peace Corps volunteers support my assertion. And the value of learning these skills in college lies in the fact that a classroom and a campus provide somewhat neutral ground for talk, reading, social experiences, and personal introspection.

7. If you were to address diversity issues, then should you be expected to draw up a master plan for what the campus will do? We couldn't be presidents if we didn't believe in planning. But this is a case where

the process of planning, and more specifically the process of inviting many people on campus to examine what is happening now and what should be changed for the future, may be far more valuable than a finished, written plan. On our campus, our plan for diversity is still considered a draft that needs more work. We may continue in that mode for a long time. I think one thing can be said with assurance. The important, and hopefully irreversible, step is to increase the number of ethnic minority students on your campus. As you well know, this must be done with an eye toward student success, both in terms of the interests and skills the students bring and the types of efforts the campus will make to increase their chances of success, especially just before and during their first year. But once the composition of the student body changes, a whole series of issues will come into bolder relief.

8. This brings us to one of your concerns that really struck home with me: the awkwardness, the discomfort, and even the pain that accompanies the achievement of diversity. I very much doubt that there is one person on my campus that hasn't had some anxiety over the changes we are going through. There are days when I'd much rather manage a bookstore than be president of this college, and diversity has furnished a significant proportion of those very tough days. An increased degree of openness about racial and ethnic issues has led to insecurities and to injuries, real or imagined, that would otherwise not have occurred.

Yes, there are now more ethnically and racially specific groups on campus and that has affected the politics of the campus and the haggling over resources. But those groups also bring new and fresh voices to our decision-making process, and the fact that they are organized means that I know whom to call. One step that has helped me is to form a standing advisory committee that reflects the diversity of the campus, or at least tries to. I selected thoughtful people who really want to bring this campus together. In forming the group, we weren't quite so attentive to formal positions and titles as we often are—a White, male security guard and a Latina secretary are among the more effective members of the group! I meet with this group regularly, but I don't chair it. We know our collective job is to keep ourselves informed as to what is happening on campus, pose new issues for discussion, and brainstorm possible solutions. In effect, the members of this group help me set the agenda for the more formally constituted decision-making groups on campus and add to the range of voices saying that these issues are not just for the president to address.

You mentioned that there have been several racial incidents on your campus. I think we differ on how we view such incidents. I don't like lawsuits or inflammatory newspaper stories any more than you do. But incidents, and the controversy they kick up, can provide moments where we can all learn something important. Last year we had a serious controversy over a comment made by a faculty member to an Asian student in a chemistry lab. The student was so upset that she went home, and her friends and the Asian Student Association appeared in my office. The student perceived the comment to be a racial slur, but the faculty member insisted that the student had misinterpreted what had been said. We invited the student back to campus and had a meeting with her, the faculty member, and the department chair. The faculty member learned something about the pressures, including family pressures, on that student, as well as the fact that certain words carry many meanings, and the student learned something about being more assertive in asking what the faculty member meant by the comment. She also learned that the faculty member really cared about her and her academic success. We then called an open meeting in the department, with the faculty member and student present to explain what had happened. We discussed what we could learn for the future from what had happened.

In one sense, we made more of the incident than we needed to, and the department meeting was reported, almost accurately, by the campus paper. But we did so because we saw the incident more as an opportunity to learn some things than as an embarrassment to be hidden. And, by the way, I urge caution in having lawyers call the shots in such circumstances. In this case, our attorney advised me not to have the department chair call the student at home for fear that the chair would say something that could be used against us in a lawsuit! I'm glad we dealt with the case as educators and not as potential litigants.

Well, all of this is more than you wanted to hear. Please know that I don't think I know the answers. As usual, the more I learn, the more I realize what I don't know. But, before closing, I want to get back to my earlier statement that I wouldn't press you to exert leadership on diversity issues as I pressed another president a while back. I don't press you because part of my reason for pushing these issues is selfish. After my first two years in office, I could have said what you say: my time was spent entirely on money, buildings, visibility, and prestige, because that's what trustees, faculty, and fellow administrators seemed to expect of me. I woke up one day to realize that my behavior was designed to keep everyone happy and to make sure that I stayed president. But I came into higher education because I believed in certain values and some of those values are tied up with what we now call diversity.

Do campus leaders other than presidents face the same issues? In the same form?

My conclusion was that I needed to raise some of these issues because the job could only be meaningful to me if I did. But that was only part of it. I also concluded that these issues really were central to the future of my campus. It took both ingredients to get me going. My sense is that "presidential leadership" on diversity only works when both of those elements are present—both personal commitment and a vision of the future of the campus. I can't speak for you and your campus with respect to either of them. I'll close while expressing the hope that we can talk more about all of this soon.

BACKGROUND ESSAY

**"I didn't become a college president to build buildings. I could
have become a savings and loan executive to do that.
I became a college president to build bridges—
among people who are there to learn,
among disciplines, among
generations."**

A college president who sees his or her vocation as this kind of bridge
building will find it hard not to invest an important part of his or her
leadership abilities in charting a course for diversity
on campus. It will be a large part of the excitement of
the job, involving the college president with other
leaders on campus in discovering talent and making
the institution more alive intellectually.

When people think of leadership in colleges and universities, they tend most often to think of the role of
chief executive officer. There are good reasons for this:
a president represents the entire institution in dealing
with its trustees and also embodies the authority of the
trustees in day-to-day administrative decisions. These
relationships place the president "out front" when the
institution reflects on its mission, resources, and fu-
ture. It has been an American tradition that this "out front" position calls
for and demands respect for presidential formulations of policy and

> ## Voice
>
> *"If there are no people of
> color—if there are no
> women—on the president's
> or chancellor's executive
> team, no amount of rhetoric
> will obscure this deficiency.
> People in organizations not
> only listen to whatever lead-
> ers say, they watch clearly
> what is done."*
>
> *(A university president)*

aspirations for the in-
stitution as a whole and
for its educational pur-
poses. A constructive
adaptation to diversity
will call for such vision
in the years ahead.

The college presidency
characteristically im-
pacts diversity both di-
rectly and indirectly as
shown in the diagram
to the right.

Presidential skills are
engaged directly in
planning and imple-
menting the college's

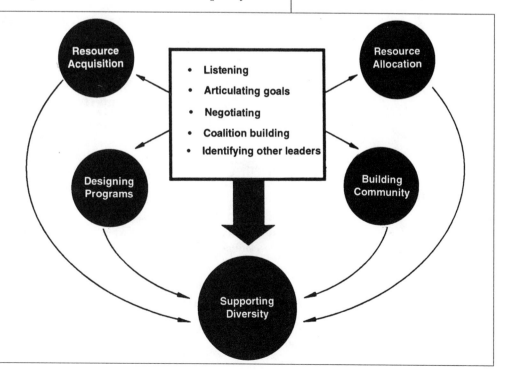

approach to diversity. The president is also involved in acquiring and allocating resources through the institution's budget process and in dealing with issues of educational program and community. Agenda setting, guidance, and bridge building in these areas can also be in the service of diversity. Further, a president is called upon to be the institution's ambassador in portraying these efforts to external constituencies.

But presidents are by no means the only leaders in academic communities. The multiplicity of leadership roles in American institutions is one of their greatest assets. It is a multiplicity that protects autonomy, encourages innovation, trains for statesmanship, and allows for the benefits of a loyal opposition. Any (and sometimes all) of these virtues may be needed for successful achievement of a diverse academic community. No level or type of leadership can be ignored as a resource.

- Deans can lead in discovering opportunities for appointing more diverse faculty.

- Academic vice-presidents can lead in giving scope to multicultural programs.

- Faculty can lead in creating student work groups that contain persons of different ethnicities.

- Student affairs personnel can lead in monitoring campus climate for all students and proposing steps to improve it.

- Residence hall staff can lead in bringing students together in discussions and activities that support diversity.

- Student leaders can take steps to ensure that students of all ethnic backgrounds feel welcome and that diversity issues become part of the agenda of the appropriate student organizations.

- Admissions staff can lead in finding new avenues for recruiting and enrolling students from families with no tradition of college attendance.

Some important leadership roles arise from context and circumstance rather than formal designation or job description. A teaching assistant in a freshman course may stumble upon a remarkably successful way to teach students to write better. An editor of the student newspaper may see a better way to increase the range of coverage of student organizations, or may point out in an editorial how an improvement in support for minority students does, or could, benefit students in general. These are genuine and important leadership opportunities, even if not ex officio. There is a risk that they will not be seen as opportunities, or that they will be dismissed as trivial or beyond the boundaries of a person's role. Although it is important for college presidents and other senior administrators to set a tone and to formulate policies that unify and mobilize support, it is important also that this kind of ex officio leadership not be seen as preempting the field.

Trustees also have an indispensable leadership role. Most trustees know they should not attempt day-to-day management and decision making and view their role instead as providing guidance, expertise, and support. But there is scope for trustee leadership all the same. Trustees can immeasurably strengthen a president's position in making diversity a priority for the institution by keeping diversity high on their agenda, by ensuring the permanence of the institution's commitment and support, by running interference with influential external constituencies, and, not least, by insisting upon a diverse membership for the board itself.

Especially important is faculty leadership. Most vitally, this is intellectual leadership. Such leadership is needed to connect a vision of the institution's mission, the changing nature of a number of disciplines, and the reality of a diverse larger society. If faculty take such leadership, diversity will be the source of exciting intellectual challenges. If they do not, if they leave diversity to be solely a concern of administrators and staff, any program or effort on behalf of diversity is likely to stumble and, perhaps, even fail.

Especially important is faculty leadership. Most vitally, this is intellectual leadership.

Trustees, administrators, faculty, staff, and students who are themselves members of ethnic minorities or women often face a special problem in investing their leadership in diversity concerns. Their motivation to do so is often strong, arising from personal experience, yet they often feel that it should not be their job to do so just because of their ethnicity or gender. They understandably feel that diversity concerns should belong not to them exclusively, but to the whole institution and all its leaders.

A difficulty for almost all kinds and levels of leadership is the need to make trade-off choices. In most cases, people who lead on diversity issues can do so only because they have acquired influence as people who are looked to for leadership in connection with a wide range of campus concerns. These leaders must decide how much energy they should invest in diversity matters as distinct from other priorities.

Ideally, these choices would be based on the importance of a successful institutional adaptation to diversity relative to the importance of other concerns. Diversity could well rank high in such an assessment. There are, however, hazards in leading on diversity issues that can make this judgment difficult. Leadership on diversity can call for the expenditure of considerable energy, even when things go well. It can demand even

---

Leadership on diversity can call for the expenditure of considerable energy, even when things go well. It can demand even more energy when things go badly.

---

more energy when things go badly—when an "incident" occurs, when opposition materializes where it was least expected, when programs are criticized unfairly or prematurely. Those who lead on diversity can at times lose the valued support and friendship of colleagues. Betrayals are not unknown and may have to be accepted in silence. Leaders may find themselves immersed in ideological controversies, and pressured into taking positions on issues they feel are entirely beside the point. They may become discouraged and burnt-out. Nor are the costs all personal. There are risks that division and partisanship will damage precisely the sense of community an effort on behalf of diversity is intended to enhance.

Good leaders are realists and know these things. The people they lead would do well to be realists, too. It would often help if constituents were slower in offering reflexive criticism and quicker in offering imaginative support. All parties, leaders and constituent groups, need to bear in mind the nature of colleges and universities as organizations: they are organizations in which all parties have some power but none has great power. The role of leadership tends, therefore, to be one of building inclusive coalitions that can work together to accomplish a task and then dissolve without a legacy of rancor that would make it difficult to form new coalitions for other purposes. At large institutions there is also a need to bridge intra-institutional distances: schools and departments may be like villages separated by forests, marshes, or mountains, rather than like parts of a neighborhood in daily perceived interdependence.

The skills and qualities that make leaders effective in other areas are those that serve them well in building and sustaining support for diversity efforts. For example, the most effective leaders in a college or university are often the best negotiators, and this will be as true in seeking common ground on diversity matters as in other areas. Knowing when to compromise (and when not) can

Thought Experiment

DEALING WITH A DEFICIT

The president of U State University is facing a large budget deficit. She believes that an across-the-board cut of 5 percent in all controllable programs will be fair and acceptable to faculty, but she would like to make an exception in favor of the programs for a successful adaptation to ethnic diversity, which she pushed through last year when the financial outlook was brighter.

1. How should she decide whether to make an exception?

2. Who should be consulted and how?

3. What would be the persuasive arguments for and against such an exception on your campus?

be a vital skill, along with the creativity to devise acceptable solutions to apparently irreconcilable claims.

Similarly, openness and candor are valuable leadership qualities on most academic issues, and no less on issues of diversity. A secretive or manipulative president, dean, or department chair risks losing the broad active participation in diversity efforts that can lead to success. Humor and stoicism are useful qualities, in diversity matters as elsewhere in academic life.

Tactics, as well as skills, that leaders have used in other contexts can help in diversity matters also. Such tactics include

1. recognizing circumstances that make the leader a "gift" of an opportunity to begin or extend a diversity effort

2. accepting small opportunities as well as large

3. choosing goals for early efforts that promise early success

4. making much of common ground among rivals and factions, even if the common ground is initially small

5. using even very unpleasant incidents as opportunities to focus attention on differing perceptions and shared values

6. building upon existing patterns of collaboration

7. making clear that confrontation, although a last resort, is not ruled out

The task of narrowing the gap between words and deeds is one of the most challenging responsibilities of academic leadership in carrying through a diversity agenda. In an academic community, words have a special power. Their validity is also exposed to special scrutiny. The

---

The right words, and the right occasions to employ those words, are indispensable for mobilizing support for diversity.

---

right words, and the right occasions to employ those words, are indispensable for mobilizing support for diversity. The words are often utopian words, which envision the kind of academic community the institution wants to be. But words also create very concrete expectations about building a community in which all students can succeed and in which routine relationships are not shadowed by prejudice. A college president can make an address on the nature of intellectual excellence without expecting his hearers to translate its terms immediately into tenure requirements. By contrast, an academic leader who speaks on the goals of diversity is expected to have concrete steps very much in mind.

Thought Experiment

LEADERSHIP ON TOUGH ISSUES

Because salaries at College V are very low, the president is convinced that the only way the college can hope to recruit enough minority faculty to meet its goals will be to pay the recruits several thousand dollars more, on average, than Anglo faculty of similar rank and qualifications are paid.

1. Is this assumption valid at your institution?

2. What is the best case for and against such salary differentials?

3. What factors outside the domain of salaries attract and retain faculty at your campus?

REFERENCES AND RESOURCES

Arciniega, T. "The Nature and Importance of Minority Leaders in the Decade Ahead." *AAHE Bulletin* (June 1990): 12+.

Botstein, L. "The Undergraduate Curriculum and the Issue of Race." In *The Racial Crisis in American Higher Education,* edited by Philip G. Altbach and Kofi Lomotey, 89–105. Albany, NY: State University of New York Press, c1991.

Chaffee, E. E., and Tierney, W. G. *Collegiate Culture and Leadership Strategies.* Phoenix, AZ: American Council on Education/Oryx Press, 1988.

Green, M. F., ed. *Minorities on Campus: A Handbook for Enhancing Diversity.* Washington, DC: American Council on Education, 1989.

8

PLANNING AND CONDUCTING DISCUSSIONS OF ETHNIC DIVERSITY

INTRODUCTION

This section offers suggestions intended to be useful in planning and conducting organized discussions of ethnic diversity. The advice deals with times, places, formats, ground rules, and selection of materials for such discussions.

One can imagine a possible reaction to an invitation to attend an institutional retreat on ethnic diversity in higher education: "If I go, I will probably learn something. If I go, I can try out some of my ideas on other people ... But, if I go, people may try to reprogram me ideologically. And where will my peaceful life be, if I make one false step in speaking about diversity?"

One can imagine also what might actually happen at the retreat: "Here I am getting to know pretty well a group of people I scarcely knew by name, if that. They are listening to me. *I* am listening to *them*. This is personal and practical. Dare I admit that this subject is *interesting*? That I am actually *enjoying* myself?"

This section is included with these discussion materials to suggest ways to make this kind of positive outcome more likely—to come closer to a real meeting of minds in open discussion and to get around, over, or through the kinds of misgivings and inhibitions about discussing diversity that are all too common on campus.

The emphasis here on open and exploratory discussion raises the question of *what counts* as good discussion. Several criteria are worth bearing in mind:

1. Are people talking about what seems to them genuinely important?

2. Do people respond in ways that show that they are really listening?

3. Are people expressing themselves in more than usually candid ways, because they sense that the other participants are respectful and reflective listeners, even if they are inclined to disagree?

4. Are difficult issues being discussed for the first time or in a more constructive way than usual?

5. Does the discussion "take off" with successive speakers bringing forth observations that build on those that have gone before?

6. Does the discussion seem to point in the direction of new areas of agreement, even if the terms of that agreement would be very hard to formulate?

7. Do members of the group show an inclination to prolong discussions, to meet again, or to find a way to involve others in similar discussions?

This volume is in no way intended as a textbook to be read from beginning to end. Those who organize discussions may want to read most of the volume in order to select a subset of materials for use, but participants in a discussion group well might not. The materials are divided into seven topics, mainly to make appropriate materials easier to find. It may be that a given piece raises an issue under another topic, and a discussion group may find the second issue more worth discussing. For example, the case of Lee Jones in the section on Student Development and Ethnic Identity (see p. 80) can turn out to be most useful in initiating a discussion of faculty attitudes and behavior. We have seen this happen. Similar shifts of focus also can occur with the thought experiments, although these tend to be more narrowly targeted on particular questions. In general, a discussion leader should feel no obligation to "stick to the text" and its structure. The materials presented here may be reproduced (for the purposes and to the extent stated in the permissions statement on the copyright page), reordered, and interspersed with materials developed by others.

As the title of these materials makes clear, their focus is on issues of *ethnic* diversity. This is but one dimension of the diversity now present on American campuses. There are differences of gender, socioeconomic class, sexual orientation, disability, and religion that also challenge the capacity of academic communities to be genuinely inclusive, education- ally effective, and responsive to the needs of our democratic society. The focus of these materials on matters of ethnic diversity represents an effort to avoid the diffuseness that treating all these differences together would entail. The intention is not at all to slight the seriousness of finding appropriate responses to these other dimensions of diversity.

A CORE DISCUSSION GROUP

Each campus must decide for itself how it wants to engage the issues of diversity and how it wants to use organized discussion to further that engagement. The advice offered in this section is intended to be of use in organizing many kinds of group discussions. One kind of discussion group should be highlighted, however, because a number of institutions seem to be moving in the direction of creating one. This kind of discussion group is a continuing core group of people, perhaps very informally constituted, who keep track of diversity efforts generally, monitor campus climate on the topic, and anticipate opportunities and problems. Such a core discussion group should, arguably, include top campus leaders, but it should also include others who, without belonging ex officio, are especially thoughtful about such issues, have some standing as representatives of various constituencies, or possess special opportunities for awareness of emerging issues on campus.

The usefulness of such a group is not in making the case of advocacy groups, important as advocacy may be. Nor is its function to "manage" crises that may occur. Rather, the tasks of such a group are to be informed, to educate its members, to reflect, and to provide counsel to those willing to listen. The group would eventually lose some of its ability to perform these tasks if it were assigned responsibility to supervise programs, produce written reports, or make official recommendations as a group. The purpose of a core discussion group is to build a foundation for constructive communication about diversity matters so that the institution's engagement of diversity will ultimately be based on campuswide understanding, enabling the institution to respond with secure conviction to particular demands or crises.

Where such a core group is brought together, it is especially important that the members of the group achieve the kind of mutual understanding and easy communication that a full and candid discussion of diversity matters can produce. There are difficulties in getting people together for enough of that kind of discussion. It is especially difficult to find enough time free of distraction. These difficulties will make it necessary for many groups who want to have conversations about diversity issues to choose times and places for discussion that are less than ideal. We would urge, however, that a core group of the kind described will find it essential to allocate adequate time for intensive and recurrent discussion, for example, by conducting an annual two- or three-day retreat. Such a retreat also could include usefully people who will, in turn, act as discussion leaders or facilitators for other groups whose members will have less time together, but who can benefit from the experience of those who have had more.

PLANNING A DISCUSSION

Whatever the objectives of the discussion, its organizers need to deal with the journalist's questions: "Who?" "What?" "Where?" and "When?"

First, who should be included in an organized discussion? It may, at many institutions, seem obvious that the people who should participate are the people who have known interests or responsibilities connected with diversity. Inviting these people to participate certainly makes sense. However, it is worth questioning whether inclusion should be so selective. We know of one instance where faculty members (but *not* students or staff) were invited at random. The resulting representativeness of faculty participation turned out to be a considerable asset in terms of candor, spontaneity, and variety of expression. The most important criteria for including people are their thoughtfulness, their ability to be good and respectful listeners, and their willingness to take unpopular positions when warranted. The presence of participants who bring such qualities is more important for a productive discussion than their official positions.

There may be reasons for bringing together a group composed solely of faculty, or students, or administrators, or trustees. Those concerned may want such a group and may feel that the common experience that unites it will be supportive of eventual consensus. However, without prejudging the weight of these factors, we would urge consideration of the probable need for bringing together people from more than one of these categories. It is only necessary to recall how often disputes about affirmative action hiring, for example, are characterized by serious failures to communicate among faculty, students, and administrators. Much can be gained on this and many other topics from discussions that include all concerned constituencies.

In general, a more inclusively constructed group is likely to have more opportunities to arrive at fresh insights than one that is less inclusive. Getting a more inclusive group to work together can be awkward, but there are steps that can be taken at the beginning of a discussion that will greatly reduce awkwardness without excluding people who could make a contribution. Thus, if it would seem desirable to have one or two trustees present, for example, or student affairs staff, or people from other campuses, or alumni, these possibilities should not be dismissed out of hand as likely to make discussions too difficult. A number of steps can be taken to lessen such difficulties and are described later in this section. In general, the more heterogeneous the group, the more skill and tact may be needed to bring everyone into the conversation.

The desirability of inclusiveness applies with special force to making the group itself reflect the ethnic diversity that is going to be the topic of discussion. This reflection does not have to be arithmetically exact. However, the presence of members of differing ethnic groups is indispensable to provide a focus on actual interethnic relationships and a reality check on presumed agreements and disagreements about what is true and important. Nor will token representation meet the need. Neither members of minority groups nor members of majority groups should be asked to be "designated spokespersons" for a group viewpoint. The variety within groups broadly categorized as "Latino," "Asian," or "Black" needs also to be recognized. A Mexican American cannot, for example, be presumed to be fully conversant with the experience of Cuban Americans, or vice versa.

Although the focus of these discussion materials is not on issues of gender, it is also important—and for similar reasons—to include women as well as men in discussions, and not merely in token numbers. Men and women of each ethnic group are likely to say important things that it would not occur to even the most thoughtful and sensitive people of the other gender to say.

One qualification to the desirability of inclusiveness should, however, be pointed out. Supervisors and the people who work for them should ordinarily *not* be included in the same discussion group, nor should students and those faculty who are, or are likely to be, their instructors in academic courses or projects. The risk is ordinarily too great that candor will be sacrificed to avoid alienating someone seen as having power over one's career.

OPTIMAL NUMBERS FOR A DISCUSSION

Arguments for inclusiveness run up against limitations on the total size of the group. There may be logistical limitations, such as the size of a conference facility, but the most important limitation is the nature of the discussions that are to be engaged in. If there is going to be good and responsive listening, if there are going to be mutual trust and candor, then the group has to be small enough that there can be a personal understanding between each participant and each of the other participants. There are methods for stretching these possibilities (discussed in "Conducting a Discussion"), so that a group of 20, say, can work together as effectively as a group of 10, but we would suggest that 20 is close to the upper limit.

An approach that some organizers may want to try is to convene a larger group (that is, more than 20 people), but to break it up into smaller groups for much of the discussion, thereby regaining some of the advantages of small size. This is worth considering, especially if members of a core group have earlier had some intensive discussions and can participate in the break-out groups. However, there may be difficulties with this approach. First, if it has been difficult to put together a balanced larger group, it will be still more difficult to put together balanced smaller subgroups. Second, the mutual enhancement between the intellectual work of the meeting and the social enjoyment of the group is likely to be impaired. That person you enjoyed getting to know at dinner may not be a member of your small discussion group.

We suspect that there are no fully satisfactory solutions to the potential conflicts between the need for inclusiveness and the need for small group size. There are likely to be people who could contribute importantly, yet whose addition would make the group less representative, too large, or both. There are also likely to be people who will feel invidiously excluded, especially if participation is seen as an important or prestigious activity. Possibly the best way to handle these problems is for the organizers to say in the invitation materials that they stand ready to assemble and support additional groups, rather than to expand an initial group in ways that would make it unwieldy or unrepresentative.

TERMS OF PARTICIPATION

Once it has been decided who should be included in an organized discussion, the next question is how to get them there. To what are they being invited? All those connected with the academic enterprise tend to be busy people, with idiosyncratic schedules and commitments. Where there is institutional support for discussions of diversity, this support will need to be expressed in official sanction for putting aside other tasks for the time it takes faculty, students, and others to participate and for finding times and places when this is most feasible, for example, between quarters or semesters. This sanction can help substantially, as can recognition of participation as a genuine and important contribution to the institution. This recognition may take the form of having the invitation come from the college president, a faculty senate chair, a dean, or a department chair. Even this modest kind of recognition can provide individuals with an effective incentive to juggle their priorities to permit participation. It may help also if the person who issues the invitation says that he or she plans to be there (and keeps that promise to the letter!).

The most important incentive for participation, however, is likely to be the opportunity for discussion itself. Many people on campus feel a need to get their bearings in thinking about diversity, to contribute their views, and to compare notes. Most people invited will be grateful for having had the opportunity to participate, so there is no need to be hesitant or apologetic about inviting people. It may be important, however, to make sure the opportunity for candid discussions is fully credible. If there is a belief that there is a "party line" for discussions of diversity and that other views will not be listened to respectfully and will have no chance of inclusion as strands in better mutual understanding, then the complicated commitments of faculty and students will enable them to find plenty of good excuses to avoid discussions. The discussion materials presented in this volume have been deliberately designed to accord respect to widely varying views of ethnic diversity, so that discussion participants can feel fully included once they are present. It is important, however, to make clear in advance—that is, when participants are invited to discussions—that the ground rules do not prescribe a "correct" position or simple answers.

Both to clear up misunderstandings and to reinforce motivation to participate, it is desirable to make personal contact with each person invited even before sending a written invitation. The following matters should be made plain:

- The goal is better understanding, not decision making.

- The goal is to do something to benefit the academic community as a whole, not solely some segment of it.

- Respect for others and their opinions will be basic to the discussions.

- Everyone will be expected to do some hard thinking and careful listening and to contribute from his or her own resources of experience and articulation.

- Participants will not be harangued by "experts" on diversity, and they are being offered an intellectually challenging opportunity as individuals, not as a passive audience.

- Along with hard work, there will be considerable time for relaxation and enjoying good company in an informal setting.

Written materials should then go into more detail on such matters as

- the goals of the discussion

- the expectations of participants

- the nature of institutional sponsorship and support

- the availability of such sponsorship and support for additional groups

- description of the place for the meeting, its facilities, and how to get there

- a tentative schedule

- a request for a one-paragraph biography that will be used to introduce each participant to the others

A particular point that needs to be resolved and stipulated clearly in invitation materials is whether participants are to be paid some kind of honorarium, or their expenses of attendance, or both. Some people feel that an honorarium or other compensation is appropriate to underscore the value the institution places on the participants' potential contributions. Others feel that a monetary incentive could distort the meaning of participation. We are unaware of situations where honoraria are actually needed to secure enthusiastic participation. All would agree that expenses should be covered, especially if hotel-type accommodations are involved or a retreat facility at some distance from the campus.

SETTINGS FOR DISCUSSION

The next set of considerations in convening a campus discussion of diversity is the "where?"—that is, what kind of setting is appropriate. The materials in this volume have been designed with the idea of a conference, retreat, or continuing seminar in mind. A retreat setting supports exploratory discussion in a number of ways. It provides a place, usually pleasant and comfortable, that is not associated with everyday preoccupations. Participants can often say, honestly, that they cannot be reached by telephone, either by their families or their offices. In such a setting it is natural for people to have meals together. A requirement of casual dress will underline the desirability of informality. If an actual retreat is not a practical possibility, it is worth making an effort to reproduce these circumstances (the comfort, the novelty, the relative isolation, the common meals, and the informality) as closely as possible, even if the discussion takes place on campus.

ALLOCATING ENOUGH TIME

Our limited experience with the actual use of these discussion materials suggests that the "when?" question—that is, how to clear enough time for discussion—is likely to be difficult. It is easy to underestimate how long it can take for people to become oriented to a common purpose, to gain trust in one another, and to see a useful connectedness among the issues that members of the group raise. Our best guess would be that "warming up" activities require a *minimum* of an hour and a half, and that a first substantive discussion of case material is likely to call for *another* hour and a half to be more than superficially useful.

Perhaps the tendency to underestimate time requirements arises because it would not seem to require much time for an individual to identify what he or she sees as the main points in a short case study or dialogue of the kind presented in this volume. Our experience, however, is that coming to terms with what *other* participants see as the main points and following up the connections among all these perceptions takes considerable time. We have heard repeatedly that discussants feel they have not been allowed enough time and that they are distracted and annoyed when asked to curtail discussion in order to move on to another topic or meet a schedule. Participants seem to regard an overcrowded schedule as being like a meal at which courses are snatched away by zealous waiters before they can possibly be finished.

A particular type of schedule crowding we have seen calls for special mention. There are now a good many videos dealing with the challenges of intergroup relations. There are also outside speakers who can give presentations that are both insightful and inspiring. It is well worth considering the use of such resources to kick off a conference or to provide a change of pace. We would urge, however, that such resources be given *their own time* for discussion. If, as we have seen happen, they must compete for discussion time with items from this collection, feelings of distraction and too little time can be severe.

In scheduling time for adequate discussion, discussion planners run up against the same problems of academic scheduling that can make it difficult to obtain commitments from busy faculty, students, and administrators to attend. The usual ways of crowding more into people's schedules—for example, breakfast meetings and brown-bag lunches—will clearly not do the job. Some possible solutions have pitfalls. For example, one possible solution is to substitute a day of diversity discussions for some occasion that is scheduled long in advance and widely viewed as preempting other activities, such as a convocation or an annual faculty retreat. Unfortunately, then people can think that they are present as the audience for authoritative pronouncements or as participants in conclusive deliberations. As a result, participants may lose sight of the purposes of tentative exploration and building mutual understanding.

More promising is to schedule a time during a break between semesters or quarters, as mentioned previously. Another possible solution is to schedule a number of times and places for discussions, giving potential participants a choice of times throughout the year, including evenings and weekends as well as busier weekday times.

CONDUCTING A DISCUSSION

A two- or three-day retreat off campus is ideal in terms of time available for conversation as well as for other reasons. It may be impossible to schedule such retreats for many people or at more than a few points in the academic year, but consideration should be given to organizing such a retreat *at least* for members of any campus core group having special responsibility for diversity efforts or for monitoring campus climate. Free communication and mutual understanding are of the first importance if such a group is to function effectively. A retreat of two or three days is also essential for those faculty, staff, and administrators who are designated to be discussion facilitators for other groups. Even if these individuals have experience leading discussion groups on other topics, they will be glad to have had the specific opportunity to experience the patterns of discussion evoked by thinking about diversity.

The suggestions that follow are intended to be useful to people who find themselves in the position of organizing or conducting a discussion group. Some of the observations are drawn from the experience of people who have used these materials in draft form, others are drawn from the suggestions of experienced discussion leaders, and others are simply common sense. A very useful source of additional information on conducting discussion groups is the Study Circles Resource Center, P.O. Box 203, Pomfret, CT 06258.

At the outset, a convener or discussion facilitator can take a number of steps to promote the atmosphere needed for candid discussion. These can help overcome awkwardness among participants who may not know one another and who may have very different backgrounds and institutional roles. One such step is to set up the room so that there are no tables, either of the conference-room type or of the type usually provided by hotels. Instead, people can be asked to sit in a semicircle without a physical barrier.* Such an arrangement can make the discussion seem more like a conversation and less evocative of territorial attitudes.

Other steps are less tangible. Immediately after stating the purposes of the discussion, the convener or discussion leader should ask participants to introduce themselves. These introductions should go beyond the brief biographies circulated in advance to say why the issues of diversity are personally important, how such issues relate to personal experience, and what people individually hope to gain from the discussion. This can help everyone to recognize that everyone cares and that no one wants to—or should have to—leave without having benefited from the discussion. It can also lead into a general brainstorming discussion of desired outcomes for the meeting.

Another useful initial move is to ask every member of the group to say a few words about the things he or she likes best that lie quite outside

---

*Seating should also be arranged with the needs of the disabled (including people with impaired hearing) in mind.

academic roles and obligations. If people discover that they share "extra-curricular" interests, such as gardening, or pets, or particular authors, they are usually more inclined to expect that they will have other things in common and to make the effort of looking for them.

All of these preliminaries go toward making each member of the group see each of the other members as someone with a rounded personal history and not merely a representative of a category. Self-introductions can take several minutes each, especially if a good deal of autobiographical detail comes out, but this time is an investment that can have a substantial payoff.

A next step is to ask agreement to some general ground rules, which might be the following:

- Participants have been invited as people who want to explore issues, not as "experts." Accordingly, the views of every participant are to be considered equally worthy of a respectful hearing and a response.

- Participants are encouraged to ask for clarification or to attempt to restate what another has said ("Do you mean . . .?" "Is it part of what you are saying that . . .?").

- The schedule is flexible and can be adjusted to allow more discussion of some topics and less of others. The group is not required to go on with a discussion that is unproductive or too uncomfortable. Indeed, it may turn out to be a better use of time together to try to think through *why* a topic is unproductive or uncomfortable.

- Participants are free to pass on to others outside the group what the important points have been, but without attribution of particular views to particular participants. An "off the record" discussion is necessary to make people feel comfortable about being candid.

- The group is not expected to reach closure on any particular point or formulation.

The group should be given the opportunity to talk about such ground rules, to add to them, and to modify them. The convener or discussion leader may also want the group to talk about the quality of the discussion sought along the lines of the criteria listed earlier in this section (see p. 136). Participants will be supported in seeking a good discussion if they agree on what counts as "good."

Ground rules and discussion criteria can usefully be written on an easel and posted on a wall for reference and as a reminder. Concurrent notes of the discussion itself can also be posted, although it takes a good deal of quickness and concentration for anyone to summarize a lively discussion well and fairly. It is hard for a discussant to participate actively and also to take such notes. A more useful device may be to have a loose-leaf journal constructed from notes of important points as recorded by each participant. These might include personal formulations, observations about comments of others, and interim evaluations of what the group is accomplishing. If participants are given three-hole notepaper, their contributions can easily be assembled in a binder at the end of the day to constitute a collective journal. People can look at the journal during breaks, add to it, discuss it at appropriate times, and use it to make a collective evaluation of the discussion before the end of the meeting. Participants should reach an understanding about discussion notes when purposes and ground rules are discussed, and the understanding should be consistent with the off-the-record character of the discussion.

SCHEDULING

It seems a good idea to plan a schedule that will allow time for a moderately intensive discussion of each case, essay, or thought experiment chosen, but then to say at the outset that the schedule is highly flexible. Sometimes the unique experiences of one or two participants can ignite a discussion of much more depth than the discussion leader had any reason to anticipate. It is a good idea to let such a discussion have its head, even if it makes a shambles of the schedule. There is no way to know whether the next item on the schedule will evoke a like level of participation or a like richness of formulation.

The opposite may also occur. A case, essay, or dialogue chosen with the best of intentions may fall completely flat, although members of the group may show great goodwill in trying to keep the discussion alive. It is useful for a discussion leader or facilitator to be able to acknowledge that the conversation is not getting anywhere and to ask for discussion of why this may be so. The leader also has the option of going on to a discussion of a back-up selection and would do well to have decided in advance what some promising back-up selections would be. A good many of the thought experiments included in this volume could play this role, as could the voices of experience. Many of these pieces are deliberately provocative, and all are short enough to be read in one or two minutes without advance notice. They can thus serve as "ice breakers," either as the first item on the schedule or as an unscheduled alternative item when the discussion seems to be freezing over at a later point.

THE ROLE OF DISCUSSION FACILITATOR

An important question is whether a discussion leader should actually attempt to *lead* the discussion. If the discussion leader has been active in convening the group because he or she feels strongly about diversity and has well thought-out views, it seems a great deal to ask him or her to accept the role of a neutral facilitator. Yet considerable neutrality *is* necessary. A discussion leader needs to watch the group as a whole to see whether everyone is having a chance to speak and—perhaps even more important—to receive some response from other members of the group. Many discussion leaders follow the practice of making notes of who has spoken, who wants to speak, and who does not volunteer. This can help to be fair to men and to women and to members of each recognizable constituency. Those who say little can be asked occasionally, "Did you have something to add?"

If it seems too great a sacrifice of advocacy to be thus evenhanded, it would probably be a good idea to abdicate leadership, even in the case of a leader who has been the driving force of the group's convening in the first place. A faculty member who has training in working with small groups might be asked to guide the discussions. Sometimes an outsider (that is, a person little involved in the day-to-day life of the institution) can be asked to lead. In some circumstances it might be possible to have a rotating chair, with each participant taking a turn for a given session. However, not all members of a group may be comfortable with this role or good at it, and rotation can obviously work only when the chosen format is a retreat of two- or three-days' duration or a recurrent seminar. Whoever chairs, it is that person's responsibility to remind participants from time to time of the ground rules they have accepted. If, for example, one participant seems to be participating as an "expert," the chair can say something like, "That is a point many of us may have opinions about. Who would like to respond?"

One possibility is to hire a professional facilitator to conduct discussions. Good professionals have much to offer. They are not involved in campus politics, and they are used to concealing their own opinions and biases. Professional facilitators are skilled at watching who is participating and who is not, and they are good at nudging people gently to observe ground rules. In their professional work, they have usually had a good deal of experience in cooling provocative behavior and levels of emotion that are difficult for other members of a group to handle. On the other hand, professional facilitators can be expensive and should be chosen with great care to be certain they do not have personal agendas at odds with those of the group. The organizers, and perhaps a few members of the group, should interview proposed facilitators and check references before choosing one.

DIFFICULT SITUATIONS

The possibility of highly emotional expression calls for special comment. It would be surprising if each discussant did not connect emotionally with issues of diversity in one or more ways. One of the most important reasons why diversity issues are not discussed often enough or candidly enough on campus is that they can be highly emotion laden. Some participants want others to share feelings that others reject either on rational grounds or as a defense against being overwhelmed. Some people will be fearful of responding insensitively to evident emotions in others. In a candid discussion of diversity, at least some strong feelings are likely to be, and need to be, brought out. Yet, a very high level of emotion can intimidate and is likely to limit the range of views that are expressed.

A balancing act is thus called for, and in this balancing the ground rules accepted by the group are the discussion leader's best friends. For example, the suggested ground rules (see p. 145) authorize the discussion facilitator to respond to an emotional speaker by saying, "This is obviously important. How did others hear what X has told us?", thus inviting them to paraphrase what the speaker has said in less emotional terms if they want to. In an extreme situation, the suggested ground rules authorize a change in the schedule, such as adjournment until the next mealtime, to allow emotions to cool.

One approach to emotionally charged issues is a kind of progression. In the context of a retreat or continuing seminar, the material for the first session can be deliberately chosen as unlikely to evoke strong feelings about what happens on campus. Its discussion will help build mutual trust. At subsequent sessions, increasingly emotion-laden material can be brought up and dealt with on the basis of such trust.

Another problem that can be tricky is a disagreement with the topics, assumptions, or conduct of the discussion that an individual does not express in a timely and constructive way, but that seems to fester and come out in sarcasm, combativeness about small things, or a generalized disaffection. Sometimes such behavior may turn out to be just the cantankerousness in which some academics rejoice, but it is safest to assume that there is something serious behind it. One way to treat such behavior with seriousness and respect is to invite those who display it to offer their evaluation of the discussion and the problems they see in the journal at the end of the session, with time allocated to discussion of their points at the beginning of the next session. If there are several such people, or if there seems to be emerging a split between factions, the discussion leader can usefully appoint a small group including all parties to make a somewhat more formal report to the large group and to suggest changes in topics or their treatment. Such a steering committee can work out compromises and enable the discussion leader to avoid any appearance of dictating to the group or being sole arbiter of its direction.

Some kinds of resistance to a discussion of ethnic diversity on campus should not be regarded as problems so much as opportunities. For example, it seems to be very common that some member of a discussion group will take a position along the following lines: "I don't see a problem with diversity. We should treat everyone the same, and that's what I do. We shouldn't be biased for or against certain ideas either. An idea is true or not, valid or not, independently of whose culture it comes out of." A member of a discussion group who takes more or less this position is a godsend. Others will respond to this position as articulately and persuasively as they can, the person who holds the position can be asked to comment on these responses, and a lively and serious conversation can result. Whether the person still holds the same position at the end of the discussion or would modify his or her position is, to a large extent, beside the point. The presence of such a person will have been a stimulus to much more candor and thoughtfulness than would have occurred otherwise. Intentionally inviting people with such views to participate is worthwhile.

USING THE DIFFERENT MATERIALS

Those who plan discussions of diversity on campus will obviously choose materials that seem relevant and thought-provoking. Such choices, equally obviously, can make a difference to the quality of the discussion. We suspect, however, that choices about who will participate, the time they will have together, the setting, the ground rules, and the discussion facilitator role will usually be more critical. Discussion materials such as those in this volume are, in effect, the runway the plane needs only for takeoff and does not determine how it performs once in the air or where it lands. The notes that follow mainly concern how to use materials of the different kinds offered, rather than which to choose.

USING THE CASE MATERIALS

Inevitably, a discussion of one of the hypothetical cases will return to the real situation of the real institution whose members are present. This is to be encouraged, as many of the questions in the text alongside the cases do. The "return to reality" can take many useful forms. There will be participants who say of the persons portrayed in the case material, "Thank God, we are not like this," and others who will say, "Can you be so sure?" There can be a flood of anecdotes about things that really happened on campus that were in some ways like events in a case. There will be some people who will take a case as a warning: "How can we prevent something like this from happening here?"

There is likely to be much comment about the ambiguities in the cases and about any perceived lack of realism in the situations they present. It is important for a discussion facilitator to realize that such comments are *not* necessarily signs that the discussion is off the track or necessarily a criticism of the selection of materials for discussion. In expressing impatience with the materials or in criticizing the assumptions underlying a case, a discussant is probably telling the group that what that person feels is much more important to see, value, or think about. It can also happen that two people on opposite "sides" of an issue can agree on what is unrealistic about a case and thereby establish some important common ground.

Many of those who use these materials will be familiar with a "stop-the-action" approach to using case studies, in which a group is asked to consider only a portion of a case at a time—the initial situation described, then events up to a certain point, then subsequent events. The value of this approach is that it encourages discussion groups to focus on particular events and the appropriateness of responses to them without assuming subsequent events or the eventual outcome. This can be a very useful method, no less in thinking about diversity than in other areas. Before the planners of a discussion of diversity commit themselves to this approach, however, they should be aware that it is time-consuming. They should also be aware that only a few of the cases in this volume are long enough and sequential enough for this kind of use. These cases are Woods College (see p. 7), Forest College (see p. 11), Bosk University (see p. 58), and Walder University (see p. 118).

USING THE DILEMMAS

A special comment is called for on the dialogues, or dilemmas, included in these materials. Their purpose is to underscore that there is usually more than one way of looking at the issues posed by diversity, and to recognize that such differences can be deep without terminating discussion. The issue of realism is especially acute with these materials. People on a real campus who take sides on such issues are often more vehement, indeed scathing, in what they say to the other side. Either that, or they will not talk at all to people they suspect of holding different fundamental beliefs. By contrast, the people in the fictitious dialogues presented here obviously want to persuade others and to do so with careful and mannered language. These fictitious people usually want to reach consensus, and one speaker sometimes tries to express what that consensus might be.

If any of these dilemmas are chosen for discussion, it would probably be best to deal with the issue of realism up front. First, the discussion leader might ask for comments on just what sounds unrealistic in the dialogue at the outset, and what this says, by contrast, about the kinds of discussions of diversity that usually take place on campus. The discussion leader might then ask the following questions:

1. Is there more to be said for (or against) each of the positions in the dilemma?

2. Could there be a stronger basis for consensus than that presented in the dilemma or, failing that, a workable compromise in practice?

3. Would the dilemma develop differently if all the roles were taken by members of a particular ethnic group?

One way to stimulate discussion (and to bypass the issue of realism as well) is to ask members of the group to role-play the various positions. The charge would be "Show all of us how you think *approximately* these positions might be expressed by real people on a real campus." The questions for the group listed above could then be rephrased as a request for a critique of the enacted dialogue. The group could also be asked "What do you think Professor X in the dialogue is feeling?" or "What assumptions is Professor Y implicitly making?"

Role-playing can undoubtedly make a discussion more vivid and immediate. There are, however, many people who are acutely uncomfortable about taking such roles, and any such assignments should, accordingly, be made with the individuals' consent and only with enough advance notice so that they can think about what they want to say and perhaps even rehearse or "warm up" as a group. In performing a role-playing exercise, it should be borne in mind that the language of the dialogues in this volume is *not* the language of a realistic movie script. Vernacular paraphrase will be needed.

USING THE THOUGHT EXPERIMENTS

Scattered through the text are "thought experiments." These are exercises with a sharp focus on single issues, differing in this from the more extended case studies and "dilemmas," which are deliberately framed to bring out relationships among issues and questions about their relative importance. As mentioned before, these thought experiments can be used as ice breakers. They can also be used to help a group see how perspectives explored in discussing the longer cases and dilemmas are likely to have practical implications.

USING THE VOICES OF EXPERIENCE

Also scattered through the text are a number of "Voices of Experience." These are actual quotations, in most cases taken from transcripts of interviews or group discussions. They are verbatim, except that grammar has been cleaned up in some cases and repetitious material omitted. Most are from students.

The challenge for a group discussing these voices is to try to understand the perceptions and feelings that lie behind them. They often have the poignancy, freshness, and inarticulateness of people trying to put into words what are, to them, new thoughts. Faculty and fellow students are often in the situation of working with such first formulations in classroom discussions of course materials. These voices are included here to provide occasions for giving the same kind of attention to thoughts about ethnic diversity on campus.

USING THE ESSAYS

There remain the essays, which attempt to formulate a coherent way of thinking about the general topic of each section. These essays take the stance of someone who underestimates neither the positive potentials nor the difficulties of education on an ethnically diverse campus. The essays do not, beyond this, propound a "party line." They examine common perceptions, formulations, and fairly obvious facts and then try to make connections among them.

There are two main reasons for including such essays in this volume. One is to remind discussion participants of the full scope of each topic. It is all too easy to see, for example, the connections between diversity and educational quality in misleadingly narrow terms. The second is to give discussion participants some advance reading that will start a process of reflection that will give discussion some initial momentum.

Discussion leaders are, of course, free to schedule time for a discussion of one or more of these essays if they believe it will serve a useful purpose. We suspect, however, that this will only rarely be the case. Discussion of such material tends to bring out strong impulses to critique, qualify, or edit, down to the level of the particular phrase. These impulses are productive in their place, but their expression is a very indirect way of sharing personal viewpoints, and the process can be extremely time-consuming. If any of the essays *are* made the basis for discussion, the facilitator would do well to try to bring the conversation back to the individuals in the room by asking questions such as:

1. What important aspects of the topic has the essayist left out?

2. Is the essay too optimistic or too pessimistic about the prospects for diversity in higher education?

3. Is the essay accurate as an assessment of the way students, faculty, and administrators think about diversity on our campus?

IRREVERENCE FOR THE TEXT

For these materials to be used in the ways suggested, it is essential that the statements and viewpoints expressed in them not be regarded as incontrovertible, and that the issues explicitly raised not be regarded as always the right or highest priority issues. In the margins of an earlier draft of these *Dialogues* we reproduced a number of handwritten comments which, by their irreverence for the text, we hoped would encourage users to question the points of view expressed. These comments have been omitted from this version because many reviewers found them flippant and distracting. However, we still believe that an attitude of irreverence toward our text will best serve the interests of lively and candid discussions based on these materials.

One useful way to sanction this attitude of irreverence and to get discussion moving along less passive lines is to challenge the group, either as individuals or as small subgroups, to devise their own, *better* case study, dilemma, or thought experiment. Time can then be allocated for the entire group to discuss such new material. A little self-congratulation on doing a better job than the printed text is a useful kind of cement for a group. WASC (P.O. Box 9990, Mills College, Oakland, CA 94613) will be delighted to receive such group-generated materials and would like to add some of them to any future edition of this volume.

The advice in this section implies that there should be some careful planning if a discussion group is to prove productive, but it does not say exactly what such a plan might look like. Three sample plans follow, which reflect the gist of the advice given in this section: one for a retreat, a second for a recurrent seminar, and a third for an all-day conference. It should go without saying that none of these sample plans represents the right (or even a preferable) way of conducting a discussion, but each puts the suggestions made in this section in concrete terms.

SAMPLE PLAN I—
A THREE-DAY RETREAT FOR 20 PEOPLE

Before the Event

1. Obtain any official sanction that will encourage attendance, and obtain logistical support.

2. Nominate participants to be invited, giving due weight to the value of selecting people from several constituencies who are likely to care about the institution and about its improvement.

3. Issue invitations well in advance that convey a genuine wish to share a variety of viewpoints concerning diversity, without hidden agendas. Share what you hope the retreat will accomplish.

4. Send out the materials you want participants to read in advance, together with a schedule for the retreat.

5. Designate a person to answer questions and to receive acceptances of the invitation.

Schedule

First Day

1:30 P.M.   FIRST SESSION

1. Explanation of the purpose and context of the retreat (15 minutes).

2. Participant self-introductions: what each participant hopes to gain from the discussions, and what some of their noninstitutional, nonacademic interests are (3 minutes per person [use an egg timer and pass it around]; 60 minutes total).

3. Explanation and discussion of the neutral stance of the discussion leader, the ground rules, and the flexibility of the schedule (30 minutes).

4. Break (15 minutes).

5. A first discussion: a case or dialogue chosen because it is somewhat provocative and likely to give every participant something to say.

Leader asks nonleading questions about the situation described, trying to give everyone equal time (90 minutes).

5:00 P.M.   **ADJOURN**

6:00 P.M.   **DINNER**

8:00 P.M.   **EVENING SESSION***

One of the dilemmas could be discussed to elicit fundamental views about diversity, higher education, and society that acquaint all the participants with where other individuals are "coming from." In such an early use of a dilemma, role-playing or searching for a consensus would probably be ill-advised.

9:30 P.M.   **ADJOURN FOR THE NIGHT**

Second Day

8:30 A.M.   **FIRST MORNING SESSION**

Extended discussion of one of the cases. Although the group now has some experience working together, it might be worthwhile to go around the room to get each individual's reaction to the case—what he or she likes or does not like about it, whether it is realistic, or the most important issues it poses. Some of the specific questions appearing alongside the text of the case could then be explored. Some general questions that could be posed about any of the cases would be:

1. What perceptions lie behind the actions of the people in the case? Should they, could they, modify those perceptions?

2. How is diversity affecting the roles of people in the case? How should they see their roles on a diverse campus?

3. Could our institution have similar problems as an ethnically diverse institution? Different problems?

A stop-the-action method of dealing with case material could be adopted in dealing with one of the longer cases.

10:00 A.M.   **BREAK**

10:15 A.M.   **SECOND MORNING SESSION**

Discussion of one of the thought experiments, perhaps using the following questions: How do the characters described in the thought experiment view their situation? How *should* they view it? If such a situation existed on our campus, who should take action? What action?

---

*Those who have organized the event and developed the schedule may decide that people will be too tired for after-dinner discussions. Talking about diversity places very real demands on energy and empathy. On the other hand, time in a retreat setting may be so limited that organizers feel after-dinner time must be used.

11:15 A.M.   Break for "homework." Ask members of the discussion group to go off, either individually or in teams, to develop their own thought experiment, to be discussed later by the entire group.

12:30 P.M.   LUNCH

1:45 P.M.   AFTERNOON SESSION

Discussion of one of the dilemmas. Ask members of the group to restate or elaborate the positions in the dialogue that are close to their own. Possible role-playing and critique of role-playing. Try to bring out elements of a new consensus: Does the group agree with the consensus elements in the text? What might be a better formulation of consensus for our institution?

3:15 P.M.   LONG BREAK

A group would probably be in need of recreation at this point, but homework could be assigned. Before breaking, collect evaluation sheets and place them in loose-leaf journal to help set third-day agenda.

5:15 P.M.   BEFORE DINNER SESSION

Work with another of the thought experiments, as before. Alternatively, ask the group to analyze the thinking that may lie behind one of the voices of experience, its sources, how it might be better articulated, what problems it suggests for a diverse institution, and how those problems might be addressed.

6:00 P.M.   DINNER

8:00 P.M.   EVENING SESSION (IF NECESSARY)

Another dialogue or case study could be undertaken. Alternatively, a fairly short session dealing with material coming out of a "homework" assignment might be appropriate. The group might review the collective journal.

Third Day

8:30 A.M.   FINAL SESSION

Ask the group to respond to previous day evaluations at the outset. An additional case or dilemma could be discussed, but it is probably most important to focus on one or more of the following questions:

1.   What do participants feel they have gained from the retreat? Which of the original stated purposes of the retreat and the objectives of individual participants have been accomplished, and which have not?

2.   What does our institution need to do better to accomplish a more successful transition to ethnic diversity? What should be on our institutional agenda?

3.   What are the practical problems that will need to be solved in the process? Consider the areas of attitudes, recruitment, budget, and curriculum.

4.   Should further discussion be held? Who should be involved? Who will take responsibility?

NOON   ADJOURNMENT

SAMPLE PLAN II—
A WEEKLY SEMINAR FOR 15 PEOPLE

Before the Event

1. Decide which units will sponsor the seminar and who will nominate participants.

2. Arrange for a convenient and preferably off-campus location for meetings. Consider pros and cons of meeting at the houses of seminar members.

3. Decide on firm rules for adding participants and replacing participants who drop out.

4. Issue oral and written invitations, as for a retreat, but covering points (1) through (3) above as well.

Schedule

First Week

Cover the purposes and ground rules of the seminar, as for a retreat. Allow time for participants to introduce themselves, although they may think they already know one another. There may be no time for extended discussion of a case or dilemma, but there may be time for discussion of an ice-breaker thought experiment. Seriously consider using an outsider to lead the session for the first few weeks, possibly a professional facilitator. Assign reading for the next meeting, giving reasons for your selection of material.

Second Week

If you are not using an outside facilitator, think of some way to share the burdens of this role. Take up the assigned case or dilemma. Give the group an opportunity to range freely among the issues presented and their implications, but at a midpoint in the discussion try to get agreement on a list of a very few topics to which the remaining time will be devoted. Allow a few minutes at the end for summing up and assigning the material for the next session.

Third Week

Another case or dilemma from this volume could be taken up as in the previous meeting. At about this point, begin asking participants whether they want to take up still another such item at the subsequent meeting or whether they want to use material from other sources or material members generate themselves.

Fourth and Subsequent Weeks

By this time the group should know how it wants to use its time, but as long as candid discussion is the purpose of the group, the ground rules should continue to be observed. They should be invoked to prevent a lapse into adversarial debate.

SAMPLE PLAN III— A ONE-DAY CONFERENCE FOR 75 PEOPLE

Before the Event

1. Obtain official sanction for the event. This might include a bulletin-board announcement from the college president, followed up by informal invitations and a sign-up procedure at the department or unit level. A meeting room large enough to accommodate all participants will be needed, and *also* five small rooms for break-out groups of 15. Food service arrangements will be needed that will permit each of the break-out groups to have lunch together.

2. Check whether those initially accepting represent an approximate cross-section of the people on campus. If not, make a special effort to gain participation of enough others to provide a cross-section, even if this means some enlargement of the total group and adding another break-out group.

3. Send out discussion materials you want to use at least two weeks before the conference.

Schedule

8:00 A.M. Coffee, etc., in the main meeting room for all participants. Encourage people to greet one another and circulate. Give each person a name tag.

8:30 A.M. SESSION FOR THE WHOLE CONFERENCE

1. Discussion of the purposes of the conference and ground rules. Self-introduction of the break-out group facilitators and random assignment of participants to their groups, e.g., by placing every fifth participant in the same group (45 minutes).

2. If "important" people (deans, etc.) are present, find some way to convey that they will be participating as equals of everyone else. One possibility: have the "important" people set the tone by engaging in a discussion of one of the thought experiments or voices of experience in this volume in full view of the other conference participants (30 minutes).

3. Show a video, listen to a thought-provoking outside speaker, or, if feasible, have members of the drama department perform a dilemma (30 minutes).

10:15 A.M. BREAK FOR COFFEE, ETC.

10:30 A.M. FIRST BREAK-OUT SMALL GROUP DISCUSSIONS

Self-introductions (30 minutes). Facilitator clarifies ground rules, including his or her own neutral role (15 minutes). If a video, speaker, or drama presentation has been made to the whole conference take this up as the first discussion topic (60 minutes). Be sure everybody talks and someone else responds to each contribution.

12:15 P.M. LUNCH

Whatever the catering arrangements, have the small break-out groups eat together. If, as very likely, more time is needed for discussion of the presentation, continue to talk about it over lunch. Allow a little time for people to stretch their legs.

1:30 P.M. SECOND BREAK-OUT GROUP DISCUSSIONS

Work with one of the case studies, as in a retreat or seminar.

3:00 P.M. BREAK

3:30 P.M. THIRD BREAK-OUT GROUP DISCUSSIONS

Take up one of the dilemmas. Let each group decide whether it wants to role-play.

5:00 P.M. WRAP-UP SESSION OF THE WHOLE CONFERENCE

1. Use some device to get people to share their small-group experience. One possibility: ask a representative of each break-out group to report two ideas that came out of the discussion that were new to members of the group (30 minutes).

2. Ask a campus leader (one who has been present all day) to sum up what this kind of discussion can do for the institution and where the institution as a whole should be going with diversity (15 minutes). Indicate a plan for follow-up.

3. Distribute conference evaluation forms and say how participants will get feedback when these forms are compiled. Solicit suggestions for follow-up discussions.

5:45 P.M. ADJOURNMENT

INDEX

by Janet Perlman